WORD MEANING

IN THE SAME SERIES

Editor: Richard Hudson

Nigel Fabb   *Sentence Structure*
John Haynes   *Style*
Jean Stilwell Peccei   *Child Language*
Raphael Salkie   *Text and Discourse Analysis*
R. L. Trask   *Language Change*
Peter Trudgill   *Dialects*

FORTHCOMING

Patricia Ashby   *Speech Sounds*
Richard Coates   *Word Structure*

WORD MEANING

Richard Hudson

London and New York

First published 1995
by Routledge
11 New Fetter Lane, London EC4P 4EE

Simultaneously published in the USA and Canada
by Routledge
29 West 35th Street, New York, NY 10001

Transferred to Digital Printing 2003

Routledge is an imprint of the Taylor & Francis Group

©1995 Richard Hudson

Typeset in Times Ten and Univers by Florencetype Ltd,
Stoodleigh, Devon

Printed and bound in Great Britain by TJI Digital,
Padstow, Cornwall

British Library Cataloguing in Publication Data
A catalogue record for this book is available from the British Library

Library of Congress Cataloguing in Publication Data
A catalogue record for this book has been requested

ISBN 0-415–08565-9

Printed and bound by Antony Rowe Ltd, Eastbourne

This book is dedicated to Alice, Lucy and Gaynor

CONTENTS

HOW TO USE THIS BOOK

Everyone who uses language makes all kinds of subtle distinctions between different words and their meanings – but subconsciously, and often without being able to explain why. A person who can speak a language has a vast store of meanings in their brain. When you look at it carefully, this store turns out to be organised and interconnected in elaborate patterns. This book tries to give you some idea of what these patterns are like, so that you will become a more conscious and aware language user.

Some general theory is needed, but I have kept it to the bare minimum – about sixteen technical terms, some basic principles and some notation. No concept or term is introduced unless you really need it, nor do I raise theoretical questions unless they're directly relevant to the exploration. We won't be getting into theoretical controversy in either the ideas or the terminology, but there is no standard notation so I have invented one which I hope you will find helpful.

How you use this book depends on your needs and circumstances, but it may be helpful to know how I have used it in my own teaching (of first-year linguistics undergraduates). It is divided into fourteen units, each of which consists of three or four pages of discussion followed by (about) three exercises. I asked the students to read the discussion and prepare the exercises *before* the class concerned, so that we could devote the whole of the class to going through the exercises. I had an hour per class, which turned out to be somewhat too short for proper discussion of all the exercises, so I let the students choose the exercises that we discussed. By the end of the course all the students were able to apply the system of analysis more or less successfully to a group of words of their own choosing, and it is on this basis that I assessed their progress.

The fourteen units form two groups separated by a summary and a unit on meaning change. The first nine units introduce new theoretical concepts in a systematic way, and the last four apply them to various areas of English vocabulary. The analysis is 'deeper' than you might expect in a beginner's course, in that later units build on earlier ones. However, this depth is at the expense of breadth, and any teacher will notice some yawning gaps, such as deixis, presupposition, modality, tense and number, not to mention all those words which are not nouns or verbs! Nor have I even tried to survey earlier approaches to word meaning, so there is no mention of either componential analysis or meaning postulates. These missing topics are all important and interesting, but my opinion is that students will appreciate them very much better if they can build on the foundations laid in a course such as this.

ACKNOWLEDGEMENTS

This course has been developing for a long time – in fact, over three years of teaching. Each time I taught the course between 1990 and 1993 I completely reorganised it and rewrote it, and I think the present version is all the better for the basic mistakes I made in the earlier ones. My first thanks therefore go to three cohorts of students who suffered as very cooperative and informative guinea-pigs. Nik Gisborne and And Rosta each read and commented on one version, and showed me various ways to improve them; and a nameless student (from another institution) made extremely helpful comments on the final manuscript. But above all I have to thank Raf Salkie for the wise advice and warm encouragement he gave me after reading two separate versions.

The conversation in exercise 3 of **Unit 2** is reprinted from A. Goddard *et al.*, *English Language 'A' Level: The Starter Pack*, Lancaster: Framework Press, p. 121, with permission of the author and publisher.

A ROUTE-MAP

You can think of this book as a guide for an intellectual journey which you, the student, will make, so it may help you at this early stage to have some idea of the route.

You may be surprised to learn that the route lies entirely within your mind, with your own knowledge of words and their meanings as the only relevant scenery. The aim is not to expand your vocabulary by teaching you obscure learned vocabulary (words like <u>autocratic</u> and <u>epistemological</u>), nor to smarten up your existing word-stock by sharpening the distinctions you make (e.g. between <u>disinterested</u> and <u>uninterested</u>). Such things may have a place in education, but in my opinion it's far more important to understand how ordinary words 'work', and to be able to think analytically about them. To be specific, we shall be looking at the meanings that you give to the following ordinary words, and words that are closely related to them: <u>bicycle</u>, <u>student</u>, <u>animal</u>, <u>enemy</u>, <u>person</u>, <u>mother</u>, <u>dance</u> and <u>eat</u>. You will be surprised, and I hope impressed, by both the quantity and the precision of the knowledge you already have.

If you are a native speaker of English, I can guarantee two things. You will agree with most of the things I say about what words mean for me (also a native speaker), including matters of very fine detail. This should surprise you, when you think of how you and I learned our words – through hearing other people around us using those words, and working out everything else for ourselves. Considering the differences between your life-story and mine, it's quite surprising that this hit-or-miss process allows us to agree on such fine details. It also shows how marginal dictionaries are as a way of keeping all the speakers of a language in step, because I very much doubt if you have ever looked up any of these words in a dictionary. (Until I worked on this course, I certainly hadn't!)

However, my second prediction is that you will disagree with some of the things I say about what individual words mean (and also, if you are working in a group, with some of the things your colleagues say).

The tests we shall apply for discovering meanings are clear enough to highlight such differences, so we can be sure that they are differences in our private meanings, and not just differences in how we analyse them. But how can we cope with variation in our basic data? We certainly need to take it seriously as an important fact of life, because unsuspected meaning differences can lead to more or less serious misunderstandings in real-life situations. But shouldn't we resolve the conflict in some way, by deciding which of us is right? No. In matters of spelling, yes. In matters of what technical vocabulary and obscure words mean, yes. But in matters of ordinary vocabulary, no. Every native speaker is an expert, and where we find differences, we can simply agree to differ. What other people say may be interesting, but it needn't sidetrack you from the study of your own personal system.

These differences among individuals are mostly matters of detail, but they can be more dramatic. For example, just think how the current generation of teenagers have added the meaning 'really good' to some word; e.g. safe was one of the words that received this treatment from the generation of the early 1990s, adding it to the list that already included terrific, cool, great and many others. We shall see in the middle unit (**Unit 10**) that it is perfectly normal for meaning to change, and we shall look at some astonishing examples of familiar words that used to mean something totally different. It is important to be aware of this possibility right from the start of the course, because an important general principle arises out of it: we can't look to the past for a word's 'true' or 'correct' or 'real' meaning. It's interesting to learn that atom originally (when borrowed from classical Greek) meant 'indivisible', but this fact is irrelevant to what it means to us today (given that we all know that atoms are divisible), just as it is to modern Greek (where atomo means simply 'person').

In short, our journey lies through the uncharted jungles and swamps of your mind, and the most general skill you have to acquire is that of turning your mind back on itself – a kind of intellectual acrobatics, mind-training of the highest order. I shall also teach you some more specific skills – for instance, how to write definitions and how to draw diagrams to display your definitions. This is the agenda for the first half of the course, and the second half will show you how to apply your skills to some rather different kinds of words, with increasingly complicated meanings. The more complicated the meaning, the more helpful it is to use diagrams, so any effort you put into diagramming in the early units will be well rewarded towards the end of the course.

WORDS AND MEANINGS

1

> We distinguish between a word and its **meaning**. Both the word
> and its meaning are **concepts**, about which we know various facts.
> Words that share the same meaning (though not necessarily the
> same **style**) are **synonyms**.

We start with a very ordinary word indeed, <u>bicycle</u>. What does the
word <u>bicycle</u> mean?

Before we answer this question, let me remind you that we are
talking about what you have in your mind. One thing you certainly
know is the word <u>bicycle</u>; you know how to pronounce it, maybe you
even know how to spell it, and you certainly know that it is a noun
(though you may not be aware that you know any of these things).
You must know all these things, otherwise you couldn't use the word
as you (no doubt) do use it. Another way of saying all this is to say
that <u>bicycle</u> is a CONCEPT in your mind, and that you know a variety **Concept**
of FACTS about it – the fact that it is spelt 'bicycle', that it is pro- **Facts**
nounced with stress on the first syllable, that it is a noun, and so on.
We don't need to agonise over exactly what a concept is; for our purposes it is enough to be clear that it is a part of our knowledge about
which we know facts.

The whole of this course is about concepts and the relations
between them, so we need to be able to talk easily about the individual concepts. The book that you are reading now has a concept in
your mind, and we could call it simply 'this book', but it's harder to
know what to call the concepts for individual words like the word
<u>bicycle</u>. An easy answer is simply to call it 'the word <u>bicycle</u>', which
works well because it distinguishes the word from every other concept in your mind. Even more easily, you can miss out 'the word' and
leave just the underlined word itself, <u>bicycle</u>. Underlining (or italics)

1

is a standard convention that you will find in all linguistics books for picking out words that are 'quoted' rather than used in their ordinary way. I shall apply this principle consistently, and I recommend you to do the same for reasons that I shall explain below. We shall see later that this system for naming words isn't quite precise enough, but it will do to start with. The name of your concept for the word <u>bicycle</u>, then, is just <u>bicycle</u>.

One other fact that you know about <u>bicycle</u> is that it means.... Well, what does it mean? Whatever it is must also be part of your knowledge, because that's what we mean by saying that you know the meaning of <u>bicycle</u>; therefore it must be another concept. What shall we call this concept? How about <u>bicycle</u>, for example? No, that would be hopelessly confusing, because we are already using <u>bicycle</u> as the name for a concept that is a noun, has three syllables and so on. What <u>bicycle</u> means has nothing to do with syllables, but has a lot to do with wheels, transport and so on. It is absolutely essential to keep the two concepts distinct, so we shall call it 'bicycle' – no underlining, but single quotes. In fact, when we use the word as a name for its meaning we are actually using it in the normal way. That's what words are: names for their meanings. So the answer to our question is that <u>bicycle</u> means 'bicycle'.

If this distinction between the word and its meaning strikes you as blindingly obvious, you are lucky. Many people find it extremely difficult to think of words as separate from their meanings, so even at the end of this course I find that some students are still capable of writing things like: 'Wine is a noun and is something you drink.' This is nonsense: what you drink isn't a noun, but a liquid. What they really mean is: '<u>Wine</u> is a noun, and wine is something you drink.' (Just after writing these words I read an essay by a bright third-year undergraduate which contained the following sentence: 'Like virtually all the creatures in the "pets" category, the fox is a monosyllable'!)

Indeed, one characteristic of 'primitive' thinking is the confusion of words and their meanings. Most societies have words that are 'taboo' because the concepts that they mean are 'taboo'. We don't have to go to exotic tribal societies to find examples; just think of any 'four-letter' word. Why is it bad? Is it because its meaning is in some sense forbidden? Why should that carry over to the word itself? The point is that we all grow up in a society where the difference between words and their meanings tends to be blurred (as witness the game 'I-spy', where you claim to be able to see 'something beginning with B'?), so we have to fight against this tendency.

We are already recognising the distinction by underlining words but not their meanings, but we can make it even more clearly by using diagrams. In all the diagrams in this course, words are written below their meanings. (Think of words as relatively concrete and down-to-earth, with meanings as relatively abstract and existing on a 'higher' plane.) Just in case the word–meaning distinction doesn't leap out at you from the vertical dimension plus the underlining of the word, a dotted horizontal line will separate them. Here, then, is our first diagram, showing the relation between the word <u>bicycle</u> and its meaning, 'bicycle':

(1)

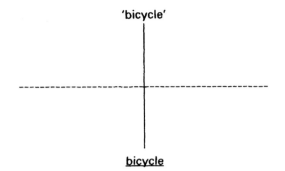

Having distinguished words and their meanings, we can now put the distinction to work in our first exercise in the analysis of meaning. Perhaps the simplest kind of analysis is to identify SYNONYMS – words that have the same meaning. Does English contain any synonyms for <u>bicycle</u>? Yes, we have at least one: <u>cycle</u>. It is easy to test for synonymy:

Synonym

> *Test for synonymy*
>
> If two words W1 and W2 are synonymous, then anything which can be described using W1 (in the relevant meaning) can also be described using W2, and vice versa.

Is it possible to imagine something which could be described as a bicycle but not as a cycle? Presumably not. But what about a cycle which isn't a bicycle? It's true that the cycle of the seasons isn't a bicycle; but that's not relevant, because it involves a different meaning of <u>cycle</u>. For the present we must just bear in mind that many words have more than one meaning, so in testing for synonymy we have to ignore all the irrelevant meanings.

Please notice that our definition of 'synonym' is quite a lax one, and does not require pairs of synonyms to share *all* their meanings; one shared meaning is enough. Nor does it require them to be interchangeable even in the relevant meaning. This is important because words that share the same meaning very often (in fact, normally) are different in STYLE. For instance, you may well feel that there are situations where <u>cycle</u> would sound odd (a bit archaic, perhaps?), but where <u>bicycle</u> would be fine. This is not because their meanings are different but because the situations in which you use the words are different.

Style

Synonyms make the differences between words and their meanings somewhat more interesting than in the '<u>bicycle</u> means "bicycle"' example. The point is that at least one of the words must have a meaning whose name is *not* that word itself. Take our examples, <u>bicycle</u> and <u>cycle</u>. If they have the same meaning, there must be just one concept which doubles up as the meaning for both words, so it has just one name. If we call it 'bicycle', then we must say that the meaning of <u>cycle</u> is 'bicycle' (not 'cycle'); and if we call it 'cycle', then <u>bicycle</u> means 'cycle'.

Which name should we choose in such cases? It really doesn't matter, so long as we are consistent – i.e. so long as we never use any other name for that concept. This is such an important point that I shall promote it to the status of a principle:

The Labelling Principle

We can use any names we wish as labels for concepts, so long as we use them consistently. The only other criterion is convenience.

I shall choose 'bicycle', because we already know that <u>cycle</u> has (at least) two meanings, so it will be convenient to release 'cycle' for one of them. Here then is another diagram, this time showing the synonymy of <u>bicycle</u> and <u>cycle</u>, and also the fact that <u>cycle</u> has two meanings:

(2)

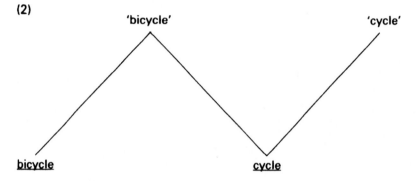

A curious consequence of the Labelling Principle is that the word and the label for its meaning need not even belong to the same language. If we wanted to use the French word <u>vélo</u> as the basis for our name, we could call the meaning of <u>bicycle</u> and <u>cycle</u> 'vélo'. But this means that <u>vélo</u> qualifies, by our definition, as another synonym of <u>bicycle</u>. In other words, when a word in one language translates a word in another language, this is because they share the same meaning and are synonyms. For good measure we can add the German word <u>Fahrrad</u> to our list, and show the relations in the diagram below.

On this first leg of our journey through your mind we have looked in detail at a tiny area, where you keep your concepts for 'bicycle' and the word <u>bicycle</u>. This has given us a chance to make two distinctions

(3)

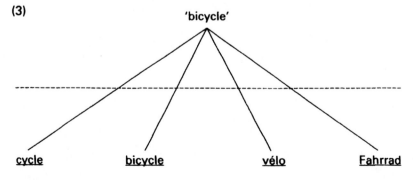

which will be vital in the remainder of this course: between a word and its meaning, and between meaning and style. These distinctions allow us to say that bicycle and cycle have the same meaning, 'bicycle', even if they differ in style; and we can even say that vélo means 'bicycle', without falling into the trap of saying that it means bicycle!

You may be surprised to notice that in talking about the meaning of bicycle we haven't used the word definition. Definitions are important, and we shall discuss them in **Unit 5**, but they can wait. We have already prepared for them by mentioning the facts about 'bicycle' that involve wheels, transport and so on; these facts will gradually turn into a definition. Before we get to that stage we have to distinguish two different kinds of meaning and make some other rather fundamental points. Our next unit is about the two kinds of meaning.

✎ **EXERCISES**

1 We start with synonyms:

    (a) Find the word in the list of nouns (in the appendix) which is the best candidate for being another synonym of bicycle, and, assuming it is a synonym, draw a diagram to show the relation between these two words like the one for bicycle and cycle. Why is there some doubt about whether it really is a synonym?

    (b) Pick out three pairs of synonyms in the list of nouns and draw similar diagrams for them.

    (c) Repeat (b) for the list of verbs in the appendix.

---

2 We distinguished meaning from style in talking about bicycle and cycle, but style is a rather vague word so you may not be sure what kinds of difference I want to include under this term. Basically I want to use it here to cover any kind of difference which isn't due to meaning, so some more examples may be helpful:

horse	gee-gee	I saw a horse/gee-gee.
father	dad	Here comes your father/dad.
get	receive	I got/received your letter.
too	also	Mary came too/also.
frock	dress	She was wearing a red frock/dress.

    (a) Do any of the synonym pairs that you found in exercise 1 belong to the same style?

    (b) Choose a pair of synonyms that are stylistically different and try to say what the difference is by describing the kind of situation in which you might use each one (e.g. when talking to friends or when writing an essay).

    (c) What words do you know for distinguishing styles? (One example is formal.) One way to describe style is to take one kind of language use as 'normal', and then only mention the style of words which are used in other ways. If you took this approach, what would you take as normal usage – e.g. in the pair get/receive, would you describe get as 'casual', or receive as 'bookish' or 'formal'?

(d) It is inefficient to have two words expressing the same meaning. Why do you think English has synonyms?

(e) Can you find any words in the lists which are restricted to use in a limited range of styles, but which have no synonyms for use in other styles? If so, does this matter?

Arbitrary

3 The differences among languages show that not only are words different from their senses, but the pairings of words with senses is essentially ARBITRARY: any word could, in principle, be used to express any sense.

(a) Collect words for 'hand' from as many languages as possible, and look for similarities in the form of the words themselves which might give a clue to their shared sense.

(b) Now do the same for 'foot'.

(c) If a language had a word such as manu, you might guess it meant 'hand' rather than 'foot'. Does this show that word-sense links are not arbitrary after all?

(d) (In a multilingual class.) Pool your words for 'hand' and 'foot', without saying which words have which meaning, and all try to guess the meanings of the words you *don't* know.

SENSES AND REFERENTS

2

When a word is used on a particular occasion it **refers** to some person or thing by picking it out. Whoever or whatever a word refers to is its **referent** on that occasion of use. In contrast, the general concept that is always linked to it is its **sense**. A word may be linked to an earlier word by **anaphora**, which is the sharing of meaning; but this may involve either the words' referents, or their senses.

In the first unit we assumed that the word <u>bicycle</u> always has the same meaning, namely 'bicycle'. In this unit we shall recognise that the word 'meaning' is commonly used in another way as well. To avoid confusion, I shall use the standard technical term for the first kind of meaning, which is SENSE. Although this is a technical term, it actually corresponds in meaning (i.e. sense!) to its ordinary use in sentences like 'He may not be lying in the strict sense of the word'. As far as <u>bicycle</u> is concerned, then, 'bicycle' is its sense.

Sense

Now look at sentence (1):

(1) Fred parked his bicycle next to Betty's bicycle.

What is the meaning of the word <u>bicycle</u> in this sentence? On the one hand we could agree that it has the same meaning each time it is used, but on the other we would also agree that it is used to 'mean' two different things, Fred's bicycle and Betty's bicycle. This is a sure sign that we are using the word <u>meaning</u> in two different ways. When we agreed that both examples of bicycle have the same meaning we meant that they have the same sense – i.e. it has the sense 'bicycle' on both occasions. But when we think of <u>bicycle</u> as meaning specifically Fred's bicycle we have a different kind of meaning in mind – something like 'the particular thing the speaker has in mind when saying that word'.

7

Referent

There is a standard technical term for 'having something particular in mind when saying a word', which is the verb <u>refer</u>. This allows us to say that the speaker of (1) was referring to Fred's bicycle when saying <u>his bicycle</u>, but to Betty's when saying <u>Betty's bicycle</u>. The thing referred to is called (rather unhelpfully) the word's REFERENT, so the two <u>bicycles</u> in (1) have the same sense but different referents. In short, we can recognise two parts to the meaning of a word like <u>bicycle</u>: its sense, which lives permanently in the dictionary, and its referent, which varies from occasion to occasion.

The verb <u>refer</u> looks familiar, but the technical sense that it has when applied to word meaning is rather special, and you need to use it with care. The basic point is that the only thing you can use <u>bicycle</u> to refer to, in the technical sense, is a bicycle; and in general terms, a word's referent must always be an example of its sense. (I'll explain this in more detail in the next unit.) In everyday usage, <u>refer</u> can have a much vaguer meaning. Take the sentences in (2), for example:

(2) A: Have you got your bicycle back yet?
     B: What do you mean?
     A: I was just referring to the problem you told me about.

The first contribution from speaker A 'refers' to an earlier problem in the sense of alluding to it. No word in that sentence refers to the problem in our technical sense. We shall look more carefully at the relation between referents and senses in the next unit, but you should be warned that we can 'refer to' things (in various non-technical senses of <u>refer</u>) which are not referents.

If a word's sense and its referent are different, they need different names in the analysis (i.e. in our diagrams). If we call the sense of <u>bicycle</u> 'bicycle', we certainly can't use this name for either of the referents; and whatever we call one of the referents, we need a different name for the other. But how many names for referents shall we need? The answer to this question depends on how many bicycles you think there are, but the answer must run into many hundreds of millions – not to mention all the 'potential bicycles' that could be referred to by the same word in future centuries! The problem of giving names to referents is clearly quite different from that of naming senses. An easy solution is to use arbitrary numbers as names for referents. It doesn't matter which numbers we use, so long as different referents have different numbers and a given referent always has the same number; so the easiest way to use numbers in a diagram is to start with 1 for the first referent you put into that diagram, 2 for the next, and so on.

How can we include referents in our diagrams? For the present our main concern is to distinguish referents from senses. We are using a straight line to link a word to its sense, so we can now use a curved one for the referent link:

(3)

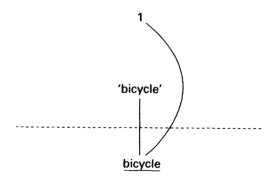

Why a curved line for the referent, and a straight one for the sense? Because we can usually go 'straight' to the sense, simply by finding the word in our vocabulary; but to find the referent we have to go by a much more roundabout route, taking account of many things that we know about the current occasion. In other words, we have to answer the question 'Which bicycle is being referred to here, out of the millions of bicycles that exist or could exist?' It's your knowledge of English that supplies the sense, but your knowledge of the world (including what's going on around you at the moment) that supplies the referent.

Most words are like <u>bicycle</u> in having a fixed sense (or at most a limited range of senses) but different referents on different occasions. However, there are exceptions in both directions.

- Proper nouns (i.e. names) have stable referents (e.g. <u>London</u>, <u>Mary</u>, <u>Fido</u>) and don't seem to have any sense at all for reasons that I shall outline below. (Admittedly the same name may be shared by many places, people or dogs, but for any given pair of people the range of potential referents for <u>Mary</u> or <u>Fido</u> that they both know is limited.)
- Pronouns (e.g. <u>he</u>, <u>himself</u>, <u>who</u>) have variable referents but, like proper nouns, they may not have any sense at all.
- The noun <u>one</u> (plural <u>ones</u>) has a variable sense, as in (4):

(4) a. The red bicycle is better than the green *one*.
   b. These cups are clean, but the other *ones* are dirty.
   c. A: Which room is yours?
      B: The *one* with the door open.

Some of these words are very useful tools for studying the meanings of other words, because they are, as it were, parasitic on other words. Rather than having stable meanings of their own, they borrow meanings from other words in their surroundings by a process called ANAPHORA (based on a Greek word which means, rather confusingly, 'refer'!). For example, in (5) <u>he</u> is linked by anaphora to John:

Anaphora

(5) When John borrowed my bike, he promised to bring it back soon.

In this case, the anaphora link involves shared referents, because <u>he</u> has the same referent as <u>John</u> (i.e. it refers to John, but not to <u>John</u>!). Similarly <u>it</u> has the same referent as <u>my bike</u>.

These pronouns give us a useful way of deciding which words have referents.

Test for referents

Any word which can be linked by anaphora to a pronoun such as <u>he</u> or <u>it</u> must have a referent, because this is what it shares with the pronoun.

Not surprisingly, we find that all nouns do, even though their referents may be completely abstract (e.g. <u>hour</u>, <u>plan</u> and <u>fact</u>, all of which can be linked by anaphora to <u>it</u>).

More surprisingly, though, the test indicates referents for verbs (or whole sentences). For example, take (6):

(6) John stole my bike. It was so unlike him.

What is the referent of <u>it</u> in <u>It was so unlike him</u>? It can't be the bicycle, nor can it be John, but it is the whole situation of John stealing my bike. One way to describe this conclusion is to say that this situation is the referent of the whole sentence <u>John stole my bike</u>; but another way is to say that the situation is the referent of the verb <u>stole</u>. Either way we have allowed referents to be allocated to things other than nouns. We shall have something to say about verbs and their referents in the very last unit.

Anaphora doesn't always involve referents: sometimes it involves senses. This is most clearly true of the noun <u>one</u> (plural <u>ones</u>) which I mentioned earlier. In (4a), for example, <u>the green one</u> borrows the sense 'bicycle' from the word <u>bicycle</u> earlier in the sentence, though they refer to different bicycles. This gives another useful test, the test for senses:

Test for senses

Whatever part of a word's meaning can be shared by <u>one</u>(<u>s</u>) must be its sense.

Does a proper noun have a sense as well as a referent? Well, let's try the test. If a word like <u>Mary</u> does have a sense (presumably, something like 'female human', or perhaps even 'female human called <u>Mary</u>') it should show up by being shared by <u>one</u>(<u>s</u>). How do you find sentence (7)? (The '!' is used to show oddity.)

(7) I saw Mary yesterday. I haven't seen her/!one for years.

If <u>Mary</u> does have a sense, it ought to be possible to use <u>one</u> here, to mean either 'female human' or 'female human called <u>Mary</u>'. My own view is that this is simply impossible. One easy explanation (though by no means the only one) is that proper nouns have no sense at all.

The main point of this unit has been to introduce the contrast between senses and referents, and sharpening this distinction is the ultimate justification for everything else – for the labels (e.g. 'bicycle' versus '1'), for the diagramming conventions (straight lines versus curves) and for the two tests.

To illustrate all these possibilities, here is a sentence showing the senses and referents of selected words in a sentence. The two diagrams are exactly equivalent, but use different ways to show that senses or referents are the same. You can use whichever system is more convenient.

(8)

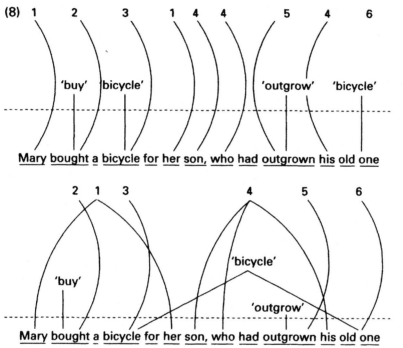

The next unit will discuss the relation between a word's referent and its sense.

✒ EXERCISE

1 Draw a diagram like either of the ones in (8) for each of the following sentences, showing the referents of the italicised words.

(a) *Fred* congratulated *himself* on the *joke which he* had just told.

(b) I ran into *Jenny* yesterday, *who* says *she*'s really enjoying this *course*.

(c) When *Bill* bought an *ice-cream*, the *idiot* forgot to buy *one* for me.

(d) *John came* late, *which* meant we had to wait.

2 In the following news story, list all the people who are referred to, and for each person the words which refer to them.

Seven months after staging a controversial comeback in sanctions-strapped Yugoslavia, Bobby Fischer has gone from being the chess world's bad boy to its poor boy. Fischer remained holed up yesterday in the Belgrade hotel suite he has occupied for months, waiting in vain for his flamboyant benefactor to return with the cash he was promised. 'I think he is staying here for a very long time', said a member of the hotel staff. Jezdimir Vasiljevic, a Serbian banker with alleged Mafia links and known as the 'Big Boss', did a bunk to Israel three weeks ago when his Yugoskandik bank crashed, leaving hundreds of thousands of depositors impoverished. After a 21-year absence from the international scene, the hermit of chess was lured out of his Californian cave last year for a rematch with old cold war rival, Boris Spassky, when Mr Vasiljevic put up a $5 million kitty in the most spectacular sanctions-busting ruse seen in rump Yugoslavia. By November Fischer had beaten Spassky 10–5 and earned two-thirds of the prize money. But not before the United States government had accused him of breaching sanctions and warned he could face 10 years in jail and a $250,000 fine if he returned to the US. According to the Belgrade media, he has not yet seen any of the prize money and is believed to be waiting for Mr Vasiljevic to return, as the banker has repeatedly promised but never dared to do. In the meantime, Fischer, aged 50, plays snooker, never leaves the hotel and shuns company. 'Mr Bobby is not here. I don't know where he is, I don't know when he's coming back', said Vojo, his bodyguard. It is not clear who is picking up the $150 a night bill for Fischer's hotel, but it is not thought to be Mr Vasiljevic.

(*Guardian* 1 April 1993)

---

3 In the following transcribed conversation, several words have the same referent as other words in the transcript. Find all these words and put them into groups according to which referent they share. (Use the line numbers to distinguish different occurrences of the same word; e.g. it(1) versus it(7).) Notice that in this exercise, unlike exercise 2, the shared referents you are looking for need not be people.

1 A: Hi. I've got one. It took ages.
2 B: Hi. Mind all that stuff.
3 A. You've got a lot done.
4 B: Colin's given us a hand.
5 A: Hi.
6 C: Hi.

 7 B: Where'd you get it?
 8 A: Holroyd's.
 9 B: Give us it here.
10 C: Is this coming out?
11 B: What? Er, no, leave that, thanks.
12 A: Is it right?
13 B: Yes.
14 C: What needs doing next?
15 B: Let's knock off for a brew.
16 C: Great idea.
17 A: Look I'm a bit pushed, I'll come back this aft.
18   Gavin and Simon'll help.
19 B: Keep out of the boozer.
20 A: Skint anyway.
21 C: It's nearly off, this.
22 B: It'll plaster back in again. Don't make it worse.

---

3 CLASSIFICATION

A word's sense tells us how its referent is classified in terms of more general concepts. The relation between the sense and the referent is **classification**, which is the same relation as is found between one word-sense and its **hyponyms**. Hyponyms form **hyponym chains** of increasingly specific word-senses, which are the basis for the organisation of any thesaurus.

How is a word's referent related to its sense? What we have seen so far is that they are different, the sense being some general category such as 'house' or 'bicycle', and the referent being some particular individual or object. In the diagrams we also treat them quite differently, using different kinds of lines to link them to the word concerned, and different names to distinguish them from one another. And yet there is obviously some connection between them; for example, if we refer to a house it is no coincidence that we use the word <u>house</u> rather than <u>bicycle</u>.

The answer is that by using the word <u>house</u> to refer to something, we are classifying this thing as a house. For example, suppose I say (1):

(1) I bought a . . .

If I put <u>house</u> in the empty slot, I classify the thing that I bought as a house; if I use <u>bicycle</u>, I classify it as a bicycle, and so on. Each word brings its sense with it, and the sense provides the CLASSIFICATION of the referent; it guarantees that the referent is a member, or example, of the general class which is its sense. From the hearer's point of view, this means that when you hear the word <u>house</u> you know that its referent is a house (even if you don't know which house); and from the speaker's point of view, it means that when you want to refer to a house, you know that you can use the word <u>house</u> with a good chance of not being misunderstood.

Classification

A convenient way to diagram the 'classification' relation is by using a triangle with its base along the general (and therefore 'bigger') category and its apex pointing at the member, with an extension line to link the two. Here, then, is a diagram showing the relations among the word <u>bicycle</u>, its sense 'bicycle' and its referent, the particular bicycle referred to on this occasion and labelled '1' in the diagram.

(2)

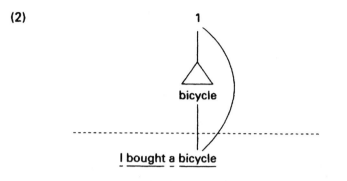

This classification relation between referents and senses is at the heart of language, because it allows us to use a finite vocabulary, carrying a finite number of senses, to refer to an infinite variety of things. This is very easy to see with the word <u>number</u>, which quite literally has an infinite range of possible referents (1, 2, 3, ... 98, 99, ... , 999,999,999, ...), all of which are covered by a single sense, 'number'. More subtly, classification allows a range of alternative ways for referring to a given person or thing, each reflecting a different kind of classification. Take, for instance, the little conversation in (3):

> (3) A: That student was in my lecture again yesterday.
> B: Do you mean the cricketer?
> A: Yes, the batsman. The genius was even cleverer than usual.

Here the same person is classified first as a student, then as a cricketer, then more specifically as a batsman and finally as a genius.

Something that makes the classification system even more flexible and useful is that the classification relation is also found between the senses of different words. We have just seen an example of this in the relation between <u>cricketer</u> and <u>batsman</u>, but there are many other examples. For instance, the concept 'student' can be classified as a particular kind of 'person', and 'undergraduate' as a particular kind of 'student'. When two word-senses are related like this, the more specific one is called a HYPONYM of the more general; and a series of such word-senses can be called a HYPONYM CHAIN. (<u>Hypo-nym</u> has two parts, meaning respectively 'under', as in <u>hypo-dermic</u>, going under the skin, and 'word' or 'name', as in <u>syno-nym</u> and <u>pseudo-nym</u>.) These relations are the basis for any THESAURUS, which (unlike a dictionary) organises words according to how their senses are classified.

Please notice that hyponyms are senses, and not words – in contrast

Hyponym
Hyponym chain

Thesaurus

with synonyms, which are words (which share the same sense). This distinction is important because if a word has several senses, their various hyponymy links are likely to be different. For example, 'bicycle' is a hyponym of 'vehicle', but 'bicycle' is only one of the senses of <u>cycle</u> (alongside e.g. the cycle of the seasons), so we can't say that <u>cycle</u> is a hyponym of <u>vehicle</u>. Hyponym chains, then, are chains of word-senses, not of words; and we need not be too surprised if we even find that in some chains the related word-senses belong to the same word; e.g. one of the senses of <u>dog</u> ('male dog') is a hyponym of another ('dog of either sex'). The existence of such cases makes it difficult to test for hyponymy by simple word-based tests like 'If an A is a kind of B, then A is a hyponym of B'. Instead we have to think of them in terms of potential referents:

Test for hyponymy

If every potential referent of A is also a potential referent of B, but not vice versa, then A is a hyponym of B.

Any male dog must also be a dog (in the sex-neutral sense), so 'male dog' is a hyponym of 'dog of either sex'.

All these hyponyms may seem grossly extravagant, as they provide so many different ways of referring to a given person or thing. Anyone who is an undergraduate is also a student and a person, so any of these words will provide a correct classification of the person concerned. Why should a language provide so many overlapping classifications, when just one of them would do? The answer is easy: the classification has to be relevant, and what is relevant varies from occasion to occasion. Sometimes you need to distinguish undergraduates from other kinds of students, and on other occasions it's not even relevant to distinguish students from other kinds of people. Suppose you are looking at a group photograph. If you only had the word <u>person</u>, you couldn't ask which of the people in the photograph are (specifically) undergraduates; and if you only had <u>undergraduate</u> you couldn't ask who the person (who may or may not be an undergraduate) at the right end of the back row is. So we couldn't in fact do without hyponyms.

Hyponym chains are easy to diagram with the triangle system. You can lay out the chain in any way you find convenient, so all four diagrams in (4) are equivalent. All you have to remember is that the base of the triangle rests on the larger, more general, concept, and its apex points towards the smaller ones.

What we have seen in this unit is that the classification relation is involved in two parts of semantic analysis. On the one hand it links a word's sense to its referent, and on the other hand it also links the sense of one word to that of its hyponyms. The two applications combine, because most words are also hyponyms of some more general word: the referent of <u>undergraduate</u> belongs to the concept 'undergraduate', which in turn belongs to the concept 'student', which in turn belongs to the concept 'person'; in other words, the referent is an undergraduate, which is a kind of student, which is a kind of person. These relations are easy to show in diagrams.

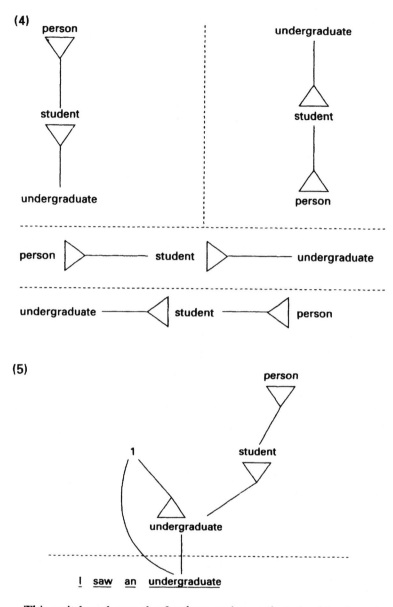

(4)

(5)

This unit has shown the fundamental part that classification plays in all our language use. Almost every word that we use classifies its referent, and does so not only in terms of its own sense, but also in terms of all the more general concepts that its sense belongs to. How precise are these concepts? Do they have sharply defined boundaries? How do we apply them to uncertain cases? These are the questions on our agenda in the next unit.

EXERCISES ✎

1 Draw a diagram like (5) for the highlighted word in each of the following sentences, assuming the hyponym chains shown in brackets after each sentence.

(a) I ride a *bicycle*. (bicycle – vehicle)
(b) They have an awful *alsatian*. (alsation – dog – mammal – animal)
(c) A *novel* fell off the shelf. (novel – book – publication)

---

2 The word-lists in the appendix include some hyponym chains.

(a) Find the hyponym chains among the nouns.
(b) Find the ones among the verbs.

---

3 Some word-senses are hyponyms of several other senses which are otherwise unconnected; for example, 'piano' is a hyponym of 'musical instrument' as well as of 'furniture'. This isn't a contradiction because each classification pays attention to different characteristics of the piano – roughly speaking, its external characteristics qualify it as furniture, and its internal ones as a musical instrument. Here is a diagram showing this relationship:

The same is true for all the words in the following list. Draw diagrams to show the classification relations of their main senses to as many

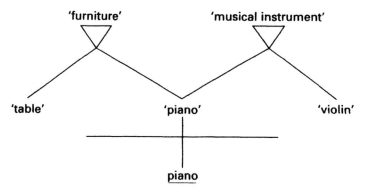

other concepts as possible. (For example, you can link 'dandelion' to 'weed' as well as to 'flowering plant'.)

dandelion, dog, knife, tomato

TYPICALITY

4

> The concepts that we use as word-senses are defined in terms of clear, typical, central, cases (called **prototypes**), but their boundaries are left unclear.

Precisely what is a student? Or rather, precisely who is a student? What about someone who is registered for a course at university or college but never (really, never) turns up for classes? Or conversely, someone who turns up regularly for classes without being registered? Exactly when do you become a student, between the time when you apply for a place on some course and the time when you sit in the first class? And when, for that matter, do you stop being a student? Is it when you leave your last class or exam, when you get your final results, when you go through the graduation ceremony, when your student-union card expires, or when you get your first permanent job? In other words, under precisely what circumstances would it be true for you to say <u>I am a student</u>, and when could you be accused of lying?

Questions like these are hard to answer, but most of the time this doesn't matter, because nobody asks them. The fact is that there are some people who certainly are students – someone, for example, who is half-way through a course at a university for which they are officially registered, and who attends classes regularly and on a full-time basis. There are others who are equally certainly not students – e.g. someone aged 3 who hasn't yet started full-time education, or a 50-year-old bank manager who never goes near a university or college. In between there are a fairly small number of ambiguous cases, such as people who are changing into students, or who are students only on a very part-time basis. Such people do not prove that there is no such thing as a student, but they do show that the concept 'student', as applied in ordinary language and as stored in ordinary people's minds, is defined in terms of its clear central members, rather than in terms of its boundaries. We know for sure that some people are examples of 'student' and others are not, but we don't know clearly where the boundary lies.

The same can be said of the meaning of almost every word. The sense of a word is usually organised around clear central cases, called PROTOTYPES, leaving the periphery to look after itself. As we should expect, there are words which are untypical in this respect, such as the concept 'odd number', which is part of mathematics. Technical terms of mathematics or science are untypical of how ordinary language works, and so is the terminology of law. In both these cases it is important to establish clear boundaries, so as to minimise the number of disputed cases. But in ordinary language the border areas generally don't matter. Who cares about the definition of 'student'? Does it really matter whether you are a student or not? For most purposes, it doesn't. It's helpful to be able to classify you as a student when you are a typical one; this gives you a clear place in society, explains why you aren't (yet) contributing through a job, and allows various stereotyped expectations to apply. And it's helpful to classify you as a non-student when you clearly aren't one, since this stops the usual stereotypes from applying. But very little depends on the precise moment when you pass between the classes of 'student' and 'non-student'.

Prototypes

This discussion has important consequences for word-senses. It means that when we are defining the sense of a word all we need to consider are the prototypes, without worrying about tricky borderline cases. Our job is not to set up a watertight classification of the world which will let us pop everything we can think of clearly into one unambiguous concept or another, but to reflect the way in which we actually think, in terms of concepts with clear 'centres' (the prototypes) and unclear 'peripheries' (exceptional members). You may see this as an example of human weakness, in contrast with the rigour and clarity of science; if so, you are missing the enormous benefits of a system which is guaranteed to apply to any case, though it will sometimes give unclear answers, in contrast with a (scientifically or legally) watertight system which fails completely on some cases. Moreover, the human system is much easier to learn and operate than a hypothetical 'clean' system in which every concept has a set of criteria which guarantee membership. Typical cases are (by definition) the most likely models for the learner, so they are the easiest cases to learn. A system which gave a clear judgement on every borderline case would be virtually impossible to learn, because borderline cases are so rare and hard to generalise from.

If humans really do organise their concepts around prototypes, and if word-meanings are concepts, this also has important consequence for the way in which we apply the classification relation introduced in the last unit. It means that A can be classified as an example of B *even if A does not have all the characteristics of a typical B.*

Take first the classification relation between a word's sense and its referent. If the word is <u>student</u>, even a person who is not a typical student can be referred to as a student, provided only that they have enough student-like characteristics to make this classification helpful. For example, someone who is taking an evening course while doing a full-time job is not a typical student, but it may still be helpful (to the hearer) to describe them as a student when talking about the course concerned. Second, we can apply the same principle to the classification relations among the senses of different words. For instance, postgraduates can still be classified as students even if the typical student is an undergraduate. Postgraduates are untypical students in several respects – they already have a degree, they are older than the typical student, their behaviour is typically more mature, and so on.

The general conclusion is rather unsurprising: *for any definition, there may be exceptions*. There are people who we would classify as students although they are in some way exceptional, and there are words that we recognise as hyponyms of <u>student</u> although their senses are in some respects untypical of the general concept. This means that two examples of a concept may not be equally 'central', 'good' or typical; the less exceptional an example is, the better it is. Equally, the richer a concept is, in terms of the number of facts that define it, the more its examples can vary in 'goodness'. A rich concept like 'student' allows far more variation than one like 'acorn' for which most of us know rather few facts. For rich concepts it is often possible to think of dozens of examples which can then be ranked according to how typical they are, as you will find in the exercises.

The existence of exceptions raises a serious practical problem: how to decide which facts to include in the definition of a word's sense (which is the topic of our next unit). The problem is a serious one, but in practice it can usually be solved fairly easily by applying a variety of tests.

The <u>so</u> test for typical characteristics

If a concept allows 'so X', the X is typical for that concept.

How does this test apply to 'student'? We have to start with a very simple sentence whose main content is 'student', so as to be sure that this concept is the only relevant one – a sentence such as 'Fred is a student'. Then we ask what other sentences can be linked to this one by <u>so</u>, without assuming any particular background circumstances. One example is shown in (1):

(1) Fred is a student, so he's registered at a university.

This shows that being registered at a university (or college) is typical of students. In contrast, (2) is very odd, because it denies this.

(2) !Fred is a student, so he isn't registered at a university.

Similarly, (3) is odd because it implies that hair-colour is relevant to the definition of 'student':

(3) !Fred is a student, so his hair is/isn't brown.

Of course, it is possible to imagine a specific situation in which (3) might be reasonable; e.g. if we knew in advance that all the students in some group of people had brown hair. This is why we have to exclude such specific assumptions, so that we are concerned only with the permanent and general concepts that act as word-senses.

The but *test for untypicality*

If a concept allows 'but X', then X is not typical for that concept.

If a fact is introduced by but, it is exceptional. Since we do expect students to be registered at a university, (4) is fine:

(4) Fred is a student, but he isn't registered at a university.

For the same reason, (5) is odd:

(5) !Fred is a student, but he is registered at a university.

And the irrelevance of hair-colour is again shown by the oddness of both versions of (6):

(6) !Fred is a student, but his hair is/isn't brown.

Thus if X is a typical characteristic of some concept C, then it is reasonable to say either '. . . is a C, so X', or '. . . is a C, but not X'.

All this has important consequences for dictionary definitions, which we discuss in the next unit. It means that when defining a word, we need not, and indeed should not, aim at a watertight definition; all we need concern ourselves with are the clear cases.

EXERCISES ✎

1 What do the so and but tests tell you about your prototype for 'bicycle'?

(a) Think of five facts which the tests show to be typical of bicycles.
(b) Think of five facts which are true of some bicycles, but are not typical.
(c) Imagine one thing which would count as a rather untypical bicycle, and then imagine another which is even less typical. Explain their degrees of typicality in terms of the number of respects in which they are exceptional.

2 The list of verbs in the appendix contains some words whose senses are hyponyms of 'talk'.

(a) Find them.
(b) Try to rank them for typicality (from most to least typical).
(c) Is there a hyponym of 'talk' that means 'talk completely typically'? Why (not)?

3 Psychologists have conducted numerous experiments in which they have asked people to list examples of general concepts, and then to rank them for typicality. They have found that people tend to agree both in the examples they list and in their ranking. Try it:

  (a) List ten kinds of bird, then rank them according to their typicality as birds.
  (b) List all the items of furniture in your bedroom, then rank them according to how clearly they count as 'furniture'.
  (c) (In a class) compare your answers with other people's answers.

5 DEFINITIONS

> A good definition for a word includes a **classifier**, the name of a more general category, and at least enough facts to distinguish this word's sense from the senses of any other words that share the same classifier. These facts are **distinguishers**.

At last we have reached the point where you may have expected us to start. After all, what is the study of word meaning if not the study of how to define words? But what about the distinctions that we have built up so carefully? You should now be able to see that it is nonsense to talk of 'defining words' in the way that most people do. Let's take as our starting point a typical dictionary definition (taken from the *Collins Cobuild Student's Dictionary*):

> (1) A bicycle is a vehicle with two wheels which you ride by sitting on it and pushing two pedals with your feet.

First, consider the contrast between words and their meanings. Is this a definition of the word <u>bicycle</u>, or of its meaning, 'bicycle'? Clearly the latter. If we had wanted a definition of <u>bicycle</u>, it would have been something like this:

> (2) <u>Bicycle</u> is a word with seven letters which you use when you want to refer to a bicycle.

Furthermore, if a word has more than one meaning (as most words do), then each definition is a definition of one of these meanings, and not of the word as such.

And second, what about senses and referents? Are we trying to define the word's sense or its referent? Again, I hope it is clear that we are trying to do the former. That is, what we call a definition of a word is actually a definition of the word's sense, the general concept (e.g. 'bicycle') of which each referent has to be an example.

24

The third way in which we can rise above the ordinary notion of 'defining a word' is by looking carefully at what we mean by 'define' in the light of the last unit's conclusions about typicality. It is tempting to think of a definition as a clarification, a definitive statement which will sharpen up boundaries and remove uncertainties; for instance, a good definition of 'student', according to this view, should tell us once and for all whether someone who could attend lectures but never does so really is a student. But we have seen that this is unrealistic. One reason is that we are only interested in the concepts of ordinary people, so we want the definition to produce exactly the same uncertainties as we ordinary people face. The other reason is that our word-senses are concepts built round prototypes – typical, straightforward, cases. We know that the real world doesn't always fit these prototypes, but we expect such mismatches and apply the concepts in a flexible way. In other words, a word's referents may be more or less exceptional.

The conclusion, then, is that what a definition defines is not the word, but one of its senses, which is a prototype. It is important to remember this in the following discussion. When we define a bicycle we are talking about the typical bicycle, and not about every single object which we might agree to call a bicycle. Seen from this point of view, the definition in (1) is excellent, and we can ignore all sorts of special cases such as the 'recumbent', a Japanese invention which you ride by lying on it and which has three wheels, but which still has enough 'bicycle' characteristics to be classified as a bicycle – witness the fact that it is discussed in the 'Other bicycles' section of a book called *Richard's Bicycle Book* (by Richard Ballantine, Pan Books, 1979).

Bearing all these three points in mind, then, let's look again at the definition of 'bicycle':

(3) A bicycle is a vehicle with two wheels which you ride by sitting on it and pushing two pedals with your feet.

The rest of this unit will be about how definitions like this are built up out of two kinds of information. First, there is 'vehicle', a more general concept of which 'bicycle' is an example. This tells us that 'bicycle' is a hyponym of 'vehicle'. And second, there is all the other information about bicycles which distinguish them from other kinds of vehicles. It is helpful to 'unpack' the definition into its constituent facts:

(4) a. A bicycle is a vehicle.
   b. It has two wheels.
   c. You ride it.
   d. You sit on it when riding it.
   e. It has two pedals.
   f. You make it move by pushing its pedals.

Fact (4a) is what we can call the CLASSIFIER, because it classifies bicycles in relation to a more general concept. The other facts we can call the DISTINGUISHERS.

Definitions built round a classifier are very common in dictionaries (though you will find that not all definitions are like this). Here is another example from the same dictionary, this time for 'student':

> (5) A student is a person who is studying at a university or college . . .

It is easy to recognise the classifier in such definitions, as it is the first common noun that follows <u>is</u>, i.e. in this case, <u>person</u>.

According to the definition, then, a bicycle is an example of a vehicle. Now you can start thinking for yourself. Is this right? The fact is that as far as bicycles and vehicles are concerned, you are probably just as good an authority as the person who wrote this definition. (And it's important to remember that all dictionary definitions are written by humans, not by God.) How good is 'bicycle' as an example of 'vehicle'? As good as 'car'? Indeed, do you agree at all that a bicycle is a type of vehicle? This uncertainty is just as we should expect from the last unit, where we learned that some examples of a category are more typical than others. At least for present purposes it makes some sense to classify bicycles as vehicles, if only to show that they are machines used for transporting people. Maybe they're not the most typical vehicles, but at least this classification brings out their functional similarities to cars, buses and so forth, and it is hard to think of any better classification for them.

In short, the definition reflects both the similarities and the differences between bicycles and other vehicles. The diagram in (6) shows 'bicycle' alongside a number of other concepts whose definition also includes the classifier 'vehicle'.

(6)

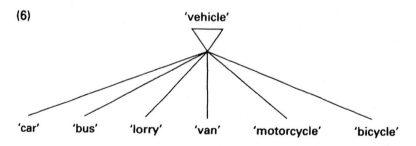

The distinguishers help to distinguish bicycles from other vehicles; for example, the fact that they have only two wheels distinguishes them immediately from all the other kinds of vehicles except motorcycles, as does the fact that you ride them. They are distinguished from motorcycles by the last two facts, about the two pedals and the use of feet.

We ought to be able to show distinguishers as well as classifiers in our diagrams, and the next unit will make this easier, but for the time being we can settle for a simple listing of the facts:

(7) *The classifier and distinguishers for 'bicycle'*

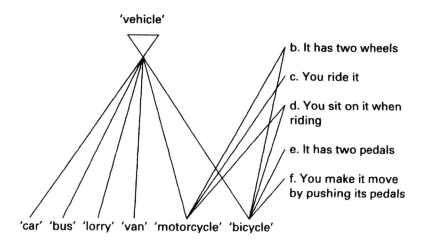

'vehicle'

b. It has two wheels

c. You ride it

d. You sit on it when riding

e. It has two pedals

f. You make it move by pushing its pedals

'car' 'bus' 'lorry' 'van' 'motorcycle' 'bicycle'

This discussion suggests two criteria for assessing a dictionary definition:

> *Criteria for a successful definition of a concept C*
>
> ■ The definition must show the *similarities* between C and other concepts by *classifying* C correctly.
>
> ■ The definition must show the *differences* between C and other concepts by supplying enough *distinguishers* to make it unique.

For an example of a definition that would fail this test, consider the one in (8):

(8) A carrot is a kind of vegetable.

The trouble with this definition is that it is all classifier, without a single distinguisher; if potatoes and lettuces are also classified as vegetables, this definition would fit them equally well, so it does nothing to show the uniqueness of 'carrot'. You may accept this complaint, but the next unit will raise some profound questions about how to do better.

✐ **EXERCISES**

1 Not all dictionary definitions contain a classifier, but many do, and in some cases when you look up the classifier itself you find another, even more general, classifier within its definition. For example, the *Collins Cobuild Student's Dictionary* (*CCSD*) contains the following definitions:

> A *vehicle* is a machine with an engine such as a car or bus that carries people or things from place to place.
> A *machine* is a piece of equipment which uses electricity or an engine in order to do a particular kind of work.

Equipment consists of the things which are needed for a particular activity.
You use <u>thing</u> as a substitute for another word when you do not want to be more precise, . . .

(a) What are the classifiers in these definitions? (Why is this question hard to answer? Could you change the definitions so as to make it easier?)

(b) Draw a diagram to show the hyponym chain that you found in (a), with hyponyms below their classifiers.

(c) Can you continue the chain downwards from 'bicycle', to include a hyponym of <u>bicycle</u>?

(d) 'Van' and 'car' were shown in (6) as hyponyms of the same concept as 'bicycle'; we can describe them as 'co-hyponyms' of 'bicycle'. Add to each level of the chain at least two more co-hyponyms (e.g. two for 'vehicle', two for 'machine' and so on).

(e) How well does 'bicycle' fit the definition of 'vehicle'?

---

2 Some classifiers are not single words but little phrases. For instance, the classifier in the *CCSD* definition for <u>field</u> is 'area of land', which also occurs in the definitions for the following words:

allotment, garden, orchard, park, vineyard

(a) Without consulting a dictionary suggest definitions for all these words, making sure that each contains enough distinguishers to make it unique.

(b) Look up each of the words in a dictionary, comparing the dictionary definition with your suggestion. Where they differ, is either better than the other?

(c) Do you think 'meadow' and 'lawn' should be added to this list of hyponyms of 'area of land'? Suggest definitions, and compare them with a dictionary as in (b).

(d) If you know what 'pasture' means, suggest a definition for it. If not, look it up and see if the dictionary's definition allows you to work out the precise difference between 'pasture' and 'meadow'.

(e) The words 'square', 'road' and 'street' can also refer to areas of land, so how should they be related to each other and to the words discussed above?

(f) Draw a diagram showing the classification relations among all these categories.

---

3 One way to test the success of a dictionary definition is to see whether it allows the word concerned to be picked out from a range of alternatives. The following definitions are from *CCSD*, but in each case the word being defined has been replaced by 'W'; your job is to identify W. All the words are in the list of verbs in the appendix.

(a) Here are the doctored definitions for some hyponyms of 'speak' which refer to occasions when someone speaks rather softly.

    (i) If you W, you speak in a very quiet and indistinct way.

    (ii) If you W something, you say it very quietly.

    (iii) If you W, you speak very quietly so that you cannot easily be heard, often in a cross or unfriendly way.

    (iv) When you W something, you say it very quietly, using only your breath and not your throat.

    (v) If you W, you say something in a strong, angry whisper.

(b) In cases where you had difficulty, do you think it was your fault or the dictionary's? Do you think any of the words are simply too similar to each other to be distinguished in this way? (Remember that if you are a native speaker you are as much of an expert on words like these as any other native speaker.)

(c) The following doctored definitions belong to words which refer to speaking which is louder than usual. Do the same as in (a) and (b).

    (vi) If you W, you speak as loudly as you can, so that you can be heard a long way away.

    (vii) If you W something, you shout it in a loud, high-pitched voice.

    (viii) If you W, you shout loudly, usually because you are excited, angry or in pain.

    (ix) If you W, you shout or sing something loudly and harshly.

    (x) If someone W, they shout in a loud, deep voice.

    (xi) When a person or an animal W, they make a loud, high-pitched cry, usually because they are in pain or frightened.

6 ENCYCLOPEDIAS

What we know about a concept includes a great deal of **encyclo-pedic** information as well as the bare distinguishers given in a dictionary. It is very hard, and perhaps impossible, to draw a line between encyclopedic facts and distinguishers. All the facts about a concept link it to other concepts, so our knowledge may consist of a gigantic **network** of concepts connected by facts. Small parts of this network can be shown in diagrams.

In this unit we shall compare the information given in dictionaries and encyclopedias, but you should remember that what we are really interested in is our own knowledge and how it is organised. The question, then, is whether the knowledge in your mind can be divided into two separate sections corresponding to the information held in dictionaries and encyclopedias.

We have already seen part of the *Collins Cobuild Student's Dictionary* entry for bicycle, but the full version is in (1), for comparison with (2), which is the entry for the same word in *The Cambridge Encyclopedia* (edited by David Crystal and published by Cambridge University Press):

(1) A bicycle is a vehicle with two wheels which you ride by sitting on it and pushing two pedals with your feet. See picture headed CAR AND BICYCLE.

(2) Bicycle. A light-framed vehicle possessing two wheels fitted with pneumatic tyres, the rear wheel being propelled by the rider through a crank, chain and gear mechanism. The major uses to which bicycles are put are personal transport, particularly in underdeveloped

countries, and sport. It is generally held that the modern pedal bicycle was invented by Kirkpatrick Macmillan of Dumfriesshire, Scotland, and was first ridden by him in 1840. The pneumatic tyre was first successfully applied to the bicycle in 1888. > > gear; moped; motorcycle; tyre.

The most obvious difference is in length: the encyclopedia uses about four times as many words as the dictionary. Why?

The reason is that dictionaries and encyclopedias have different purposes. In principle, a dictionary is a list of words, whereas an encyclopedia is a list of facts. A dictionary includes facts only so far as they are directly relevant for defining the senses of the words concerned, which means in effect that a dictionary concentrates on distinguishers, the facts that make each sense unique. In contrast, an encyclopedia includes as many facts as possible, regardless of whether these facts are distinctive or not. The encyclopedia tells us about pneumatic tyres, cranks and chains, uses in 'personal transport' and sport, and history, none of which are mentioned in the dictionary. We can call such facts 'ENCYCLOPEDIC' information, in contrast with the distinguishers which we recognised in the last unit.

Encyclopedic

Given this view of meaning as divided between distinguishers and encyclopedic information, we can expand our earlier 'unpacked' entry for bicycle as follows:

(3) *Definition*

    a. A bicycle is a vehicle.
    b. It has two wheels.
    c. You ride it.
    d. You sit on it when riding it.
    e. It has two pedals.
    f. You make it move by pushing its pedals.

Encyclopedic information

    g. It has pneumatic tyres.
    h. It has a crank, a chain and gears to transmit the motion from the pedals to the rear wheel.
    i. It is used for personal transport or for sport.
    j. Bicycles were invented by Kirkpatrick Macmillan of Dumfriesshire, Scotland, in 1840.
    k. They were first fitted with pneumatic tyres in 1888.

When combined in a diagram, the information looks like (4), in which I have missed out the other contrasting concepts like 'car' and 'motorcycle'.

(4)

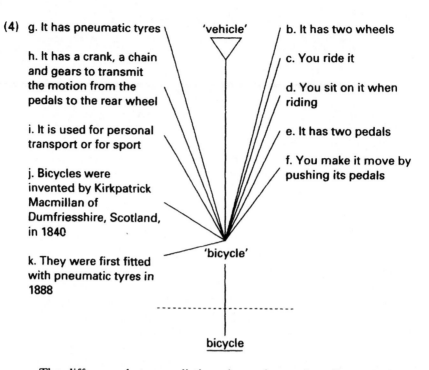

g. It has pneumatic tyres

h. It has a crank, a chain and gears to transmit the motion from the pedals to the rear wheel

i. It is used for personal transport or for sport

j. Bicycles were invented by Kirkpatrick Macmillan of Dumfriesshire, Scotland, in 1840

k. They were first fitted with pneumatic tyres in 1888

'vehicle'

b. It has two wheels

c. You ride it

d. You sit on it when riding

e. It has two pedals

f. You make it move by pushing its pedals

'bicycle'

bicycle

The difference between dictionaries and encyclopedias must be a useful one for publishers and readers, because it has survived for centuries (since the eighteenth century, in fact). We all know the difference between the two kinds of book, and know, for example, that a French dictionary is no use when looking up English words, though a French encyclopedia is just as good as an English one (provided we can read French) as a source of facts.

At the same time, though, there is some doubt about the distinction between dictionary definitions and encyclopedic information. Publishers themselves are inclined to blur the distinction by producing books called 'encyclopedic dictionaries' which combine the two functions; and you may have noticed that even the *CCSD* definition in (1) cross-refers to a picture of a bicycle, which is a good way of conveying a great deal of presumably encyclopedic information.

However, the question isn't really about publishers and their practices, but about our minds. Is there any reason to believe that the meaning of any word, as stored in our memories, divides into distinguishers (the definition proper) and encyclopedic information? Is the distinction a discovery or an invention? If it is a discovery, then we must respect it in our definitions, and try hard to find criteria for deciding which facts go into each compartment; but if it is a mere invention we can ignore it or accept it according to convenience.

This is one of the main debating points in the study of word meaning. At present who can tell which side is right? However, one thing is certain. It is often very unclear exactly where the boundary lies (if it exists at all). Just look at the facts in (3). Why should the two pedals be part of the definition, while the crank, chain and gears are encyclopedic information? Why no mention of the saddle and handlebars, which are surely just as clearly part of our picture of the typical bicycle as the pedals? Why does the definition include the rider's posture (sitting) but not the rider's purpose (personal transport or sport)?

Now look again at the encyclopedia entry in (2). If having pneumatic tyres is important enough to figure in the initial definition of a bicycle, how could the first bicycles not have pneumatic tyres? (Remember that pneumatic tyres were not fitted to bicycles until 1888, 48 years after the first bicycle.)

These examples show that the boundary between distinguishers and encyclopedic information is anything but obvious when dealing with ordinary words like bicycle. This isn't a problem for those who deny the reality of the distinction so we can take the easy way out by joining their ranks. We shall now merge all the facts that we know about a word's sense into a single list, which we shall go on calling its 'definition', but without trying to separate distinguishers from encyclopedic information. We can maintain the distinction between the classifier and other facts. We still set the same *minimum* standard for a definition: that it should contain enough information to distinguish the concept concerned from all other concepts. What has changed is that we no longer assume that this information is also a *maximum*.

You may have noticed that each of the eleven 'bicycle-facts' that we listed in (3), whether 'defining' or 'encyclopedic', is also a fact about at least one other concept. For instance, fact a is 'A bicycle is a vehicle'; but this is also a fact about 'vehicle'. In other words, this fact is a link between two concepts, 'bicycle' and 'vehicle'. Similarly, 'A bicycle has two wheels' (fact b) relates 'bicycle' to 'wheel' and 'You ride a bicycle' (fact c) relates it to 'ride'. The same is true for 'encyclopedic' facts; for example, 'It has pneumatic tyres' links it to 'tyre', and 'Bicycles were invented by Kirkpatrick Macmillan of Dumfriesshire, Scotland, in 1840' relates it to 'Kirkpatrick Macmillan' and '1840'. (So if I ask you if you know anything about Kirkpatrick Macmillan, or about the year 1840, you now have an answer!)

In short, the facts about 'bicycle' link it to a number of concepts in a little NETWORK. Each of these concepts is in turn linked not only to 'bicycle' but also to other concepts (including some that are in the 'bicycle' network), and so on, giving a gigantic network of interconnected concepts. According to many psychologists, this is a good description of our total knowledge – our knowledge of everything, including language as well as all the concepts that can be expressed in language. We can't diagram the whole network, of course, but we can cope with the little network round 'bicycle', using simple lines to stand for the facts concerned – for instance, showing the fact that a bicycle has two wheels just by a line linking 'bicycle' to 'wheel'. The network may remind you of a spider's web, but if you are a cyclist it looks more like a bicycle wheel – a happy coincidence!

Network

(5)

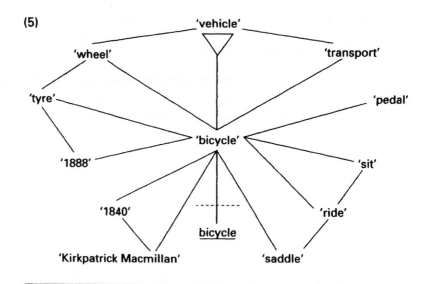

EXERCISES ✎

1 Each concept is in the centre of a little network like the one for 'bicycle', so it should be possible to build a network for each of the concepts on the edge of the one for 'bicycle'. These new networks should include the link to 'bicycle' as well as other links.

(a) Build a network for 'wheel'.
(b) Build one for 'saddle'.
(c) Build one for Kirkpatrick Macmillan (the man, not his name!).

2 Diagrams like (5) are convenient summaries of a word's meaning.

(a) Draw one for 'student' (focussing on the sense in which it refers to a person registered for some kind of course).
(b) Draw one for 'bird'. Make sure that it explains why a penguin is an untypical bird.

3 You will notice that some of the items in diagram (5) are the senses of verbs, rather than nouns.

(a) Draw a network for 'sit'.
(b) Draw one for 'ride'.

LEXEMES

7

We replace the term <u>word</u> by **word-shape, (inflectional) form** and **lexeme**. The last of these is the kind of 'word' that is most relevant to senses.

Up to now we have talked about 'the word <u>X</u>', where <u>X</u> is some under-lined word-form, but we have been living dangerously because, as we shall see shortly, the concept 'word' is rather confusing. Or rather, the word <u>word</u> is confusing, because it has (at least) three different senses which we need to sort out in order to avoid hopeless muddle.

In unit 1 we noted that <u>cycle</u> is a synonym of <u>bicycle</u>, <u>vélo</u> and <u>Fahrrad</u>, with the sense 'bicycle'. But what about sentences like (1)?

(1) I cycle to work.

In this sentence <u>cycle</u> does not refer to a bicycle, but to a kind of movement – movement on a bicycle, of course, but still not a bicycle. Let's call its sense 'go-by-bicycle', for lack of a better alternative. Furthermore, in this sentence <u>cycle</u> is a verb, whereas in all our previous examples it is a noun; i.e. the word itself has two distinct classifications. If we recognise just one 'word', <u>cycle</u>, the best we can do diagrammatically is shown in (2).

The trouble with this diagram is that it fails to show the link between grammatical classification and sense – that <u>cycle</u> has the sense 'bicycle' only when it is a noun, and 'go-by-bicycle' only when it is a verb. Dictionaries have to solve this problem, of course, and most of them do it by treating the noun and verb as different 'words', each with its own little paragraph. The technical name (in linguistics) for this rather abstract kind of 'word' is LEXEME, contrasting with the concrete WORD-SHAPE which is defined solely by its spelling or pro-nunciation. In these terms, the noun and verb <u>cycle</u> are different

Lexeme
Word-shape

35

(2)

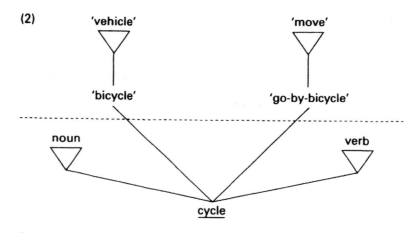

lexemes which share the same word-shape. It is convenient to be able to distinguish these notions in notation, so we shall continue to underline word-shapes, while writing lexemes in capital letters, with a subscript n or v where necessary to distinguish nouns and verbs. This makes everything much clearer: $CYCLE_n$ is a noun and has the sense 'bicycle' whereas $CYCLE_v$ is a verb with the sense 'go-by-bicycle'. What they share is the word-shape cycle. With these distinctions we can draw a much better diagram.

(3)

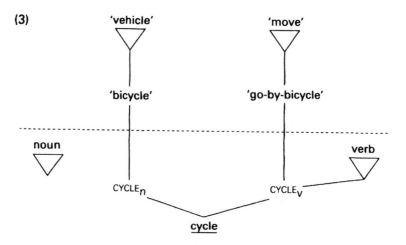

Lexemes are quite abstract units, as we have just seen. They are much more abstract than the word-shapes, because they are defined in terms of their meaning and grammatical classification as well as in terms of their spelling or pronunciation, which is all that counts for word-shapes. But the lexeme $CYCLE_n$ is also abstract in another sense, because it actually covers more than one word-shape: the plural cycles as well as the singular cycle. If you look up cycles in a dictionary, you probably won't find it; instead you have to look up the lexeme and use what you know about plural nouns. The 'words' which are distinguished by contrasts such as the singular–plural distinction in nouns, and the past–present distinction in verbs, are called INFLECTIONAL FORMS (where <u>inflection</u> used to mean a 'bending' of the lexeme). In these terms, <u>cycles</u> and <u>cycle</u> are different inflectional forms (or just 'forms') of the lexeme CYCLE$_n$. How shall we label them in diagrams? They are more abstract than word-shapes (e.g. the plural of CYCLE$_n$ is different from the present tense of CYCLE$_v$, even though they both share the same word-shape <u>cycles</u>), but they are more specific than lexemes; so I shall write them like lexemes, but with extra superscripted distinguishers: for instance, CYCLE$_n^{plural}$ is <u>cycles</u> as the plural of CYCLE$_n$. Here is a fuller picture of the distinctions around <u>cycle</u>:

(4)

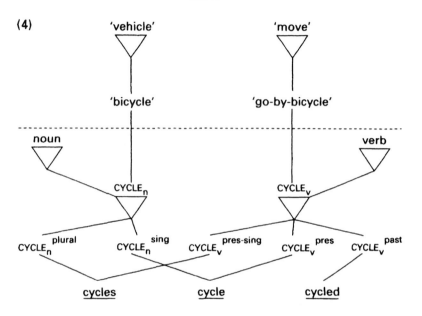

One thing that you will notice about this diagram, when compared with the one in (3), is that the top half of the diagram hasn't changed at all. This is the part that most concerns us in this course, because this is where senses and referents are located. It's true that different inflectional forms have different meanings; the contrast between singular and plural obviously affects the meaning of the sentence, as does that between past and present. It's also true that these differences count as different 'word meanings', because they involve single words rather than groups of words. Nevertheless, life is short and courses are even shorter, so we can't cover everything and inflectional meanings are one of the things that we shall sacrifice in order to make more progress with senses.

This decision is all the easier to take because the meaning associated with inflectional forms is very easy to separate from sense – whatever difference there may be between singular and plural nouns, it is the same difference for all nouns. Furthermore, whatever alternative senses are available for the singular of a lexeme are also available for its plural form, and vice versa. In short, inflectional differences are irrelevant to senses, as can be seen in the following diagram.

(5)

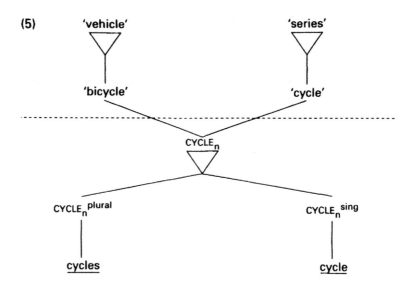

This diagram shows that CYCLE$_n$ has two different senses, including the sense it has in expressions like <u>the cycle of the seasons</u> – a cycle of events is a series of events that repeats itself. (We can safely call this sense 'cycle' because we aren't already using this name.) But it also shows that the choice between the two senses 'bicycle' and 'cycle' has nothing to do with the choice between the singular and plural forms.

In short, we have found that the ordinary word <u>word</u> has three distinct senses: 'word-shape', 'lexeme' and 'inflectional form' – a potential source of great confusion in this course. However, we have also found that only one of these categories is relevant for us, namely 'lexeme', because we are mainly concerned with senses, and it is lexemes that carry these.

One last question concerns the criteria for distinguishing lexemes. I assumed above that we could link more than one sense to a given lexeme, and you probably agreed that it was reasonable to treat 'bicycle' and 'cycle' as senses of the same lexeme. But what about senses like 'gratuity' and 'point' as senses of a single lexeme TIP$_n$, as in sentences like (6)?

(6) a. She gave the waiter a tip.
    b. The tip of the pencil is broken.

There are two views we could adopt. One is that these meanings are so different that they must belong to different lexemes, both of which are nouns. This is the most widely held view, and may seem a matter of common sense. The alternative is to treat both meanings as alternative senses of the same lexeme, leaving it to the meaning analysis itself to show how distantly related the two senses are.

Here are two diagrams showing the effects of these two decisions. In each diagram the two senses are related in the same way, namely virtually unrelated. The best I have been able to come up with as a chain of linking concepts is this:

(7) A gratuity (tip) is a kind of present.

A present is a kind of transfer from person to person.

A transfer is a kind of contact between people.

Another kind of contact is a touch.

You can touch other people with a stick.

The relevant part of the stick is its point (tip).

I leave you to decide how convincing this chain is – but prepare to be surprised below!

(8)

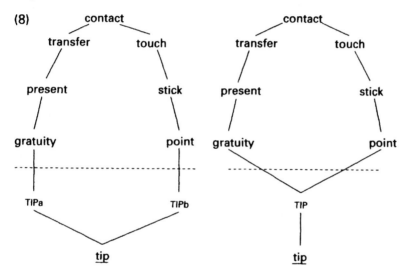

Those who use the two-lexeme approach argue that there must be some limit on the amount of variation that can be allowed for a single lexeme. The gulf between the senses is so great in cases like this that it should be flagged by separating the lexemes as well. Implicit in this view, I think, is the assumption that the division into lexemes should reflect the histories of the words concerned; the two _tips_ must 'really' be different words, i.e. they must go back to different historical roots. The trouble with this assumption is that history is irrelevant to the state of your knowledge, for the simple reason that you probably don't know anything at all about the semantic history of TIP. I certainly didn't until I looked it up in my etymological dictionary – which tells me, somewhat surprisingly, that the two senses are indeed related etymologically! What's more, as far as I can see the two meanings are linked by a chain of ideas very much like the chain I gave in (7) – and which I expect you found pretty far-fetched! In contrast, the rather similar senses of EAR (part of your anatomy, and ear of corn) are in fact unrelated etymologically. Historical relatedness has very little to do with relatedness in meaning.

The other objection to the two-lexeme approach is that it is redundant. The network of concepts already shows how closely connected the senses are, so there is no point in trying to duplicate this information in the lexemes. In any case, there are obviously many degrees of connectedness between concepts, from very tight to very loose, but we only have two possibilities for lexemes: either two senses belong to the same lexeme, or they belong to different lexemes. At exactly what degree of connectedness does the lexeme analysis flip from one to two? Nobody has ever been able to answer this question.

These considerable weaknesses of the two-lexeme approach leave us with no alternative but the single-lexeme analysis, illustrated by the right-hand diagram in (8). This is the approach which I recommend.

To summarise, then, a lexeme (e.g. $CYCLE_n$) is linked, via at least one of its inflectional forms ($CYCLE_n^{singular}$), to some word-shape (cycle), but it is also linked, quite separately, to one or more senses which may be as different as you like. The lexeme may be manifested (made visible or audible) by a variety of word-shapes, and it may express a variety of senses; but what must not vary is its word-class (e.g. noun or verb). No lexeme can belong to more than one word-class. (There may well be other grammatical differences that are relevant, but for the present word-class will suffice.) We have sorted out our terminology about words in a way that should reduce muddle in the analyses. As we shall see in the next unit, the main thing is to be consistent in our use of terms.

EXERCISES ✎

1 Draw a diagram like (4) showing the relations among the lexeme $WORD_n$ and its hyponyms that we have just distinguished, including their respective inflectional forms, word-shapes and senses.

2 Produce a diagram showing the relations among the following word-shapes and their respective lexemes and the latter's inflectional forms.

rang, ring, ringed, ringing, rings

3 Find four lexemes in the noun-list in the appendix which share a word-shape with a lexeme in the verb-list, and diagram the relations between each pair of lexemes that are related in this way.

CONSISTENCY

8

> If concepts are linked to each other by a network of relationships, it is important to use concept-names consistently from one definition to another.

This unit is about the importance of being consistent. Each sense of a lexeme is a concept with a name and a definition; for example, one of the senses of $CYCLE_n$ is 'bicycle', whose definition consists of the facts a–k in **Unit 6**. We choose whatever names we want for the concepts, so we could have called this concept 'bike', but chose to call it 'bicycle'; we could of course have called it 'vélo' or 'Fahrrad' in honour of the translation equivalents in French and German, and we could even have called it 'Fred' or 'concept-93', though names like these wouldn't have been very helpful! If need be we can build compound names like 'go-by-bicycle' or 'cycle-series'. These choices are simply a matter of personal convenience, and should strike a sensible compromise between brevity and informativeness.

What does matter, however, is that once you have chosen a name for a concept, you should *always* use that name for that concept. This may seem obvious, but it is all too easy to forget. One source of danger is the assumption that senses can always be named after their lexemes (with capital letters changed to small and inverted commas added). This can't possibly be true where two lexemes share the same sense, as with BICYCLE and CYCLE and other pairs of synonyms. Even if the sense is named after one lexeme, it can't also be named after the other; so if you blindly base sense-names on lexeme-names, you deny that synonymy is possible.

(1)

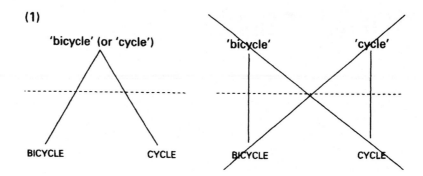

Another danger is the temptation to use ordinary language in definitions, rather than the language that you are gradually building for yourself by inventing concept-names. This is an insoluble problem for ordinary dictionary-writers, because ordinary people who buy dictionaries expect them to use ordinary language; but for us, with our rather different aim (wisdom rather than wealth), all you need to do is to keep track of your earlier decisions and stick to them.

Take the lexeme ANIMAL, for instance. (This is a noun, of course, but there is no need to show this in the name by calling it $ANIMAL_n$, because it couldn't be anything else.) This involves a well-known ambiguity: does its sense include birds and fish, or not? In one sense it does, but in another it doesn't. It does in (2a), but not in (2b):

(2) a. Unlike plants, animals can move from one place to another.
   b. In general, animals live on land, birds fly in the air and fish live in water.

Since a concept can't simultaneously include and exclude some other concept, there must be two senses at work here, which for lack of any better names we can call 'non-plant' and 'animal'. Here it is in a diagram:

(3)

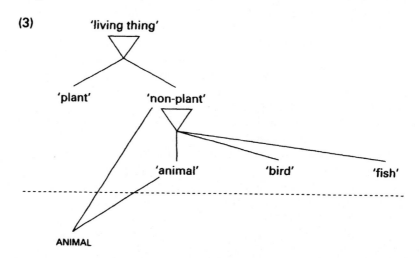

Now the point is that an 'animal' is a kind of 'non-plant', so the definition of 'animal' should include 'non-plant' as its classifier, along the lines of (4).

> (4) a. An animal is a *non-plant* that . . .
> b. A *non-plant* is a living thing that . . .

These definitions work because we allow ourselves to 'recycle' concept-names, by using the name that we give to one word-sense as part of the definition of another one.

Contrast this with the following entry for ANIMAL (from *Collins Cobuild Student's Dictionary*):

> (5) 1 An animal is a living creature such as a dog, or horse, rather than a bird, fish, insect or human.
> 2 An animal is also any living thing that is not a plant, including people.

Here we look in vain for any link between the two senses. The classifier for the first sense, which corresponds to our 'animal', is 'living creature', which doesn't appear anywhere in the definition of the second sense. The basic problem is that concepts are not named in a consistent way: two different names are used for the same concept, which is called 'living creature' in the first definition and 'animal' in the second. Even more confusingly, the name 'living creature' looks remarkably like 'living thing' (what, precisely, is the difference between a creature and a thing if both are living?), which is its classifier! Between them, these two inconsistencies in naming lead to a conceptual mess.

One of the benefits of applying names consistently is that it allows us to simplify definitions by not duplicating information in different definitions. Take our old example of 'bicycle'. If we define a bicycle as a kind of vehicle, everything that is mentioned in the definition of 'vehicle' can be taken for granted and omitted from the definition of 'bicycle'. If all vehicles are used for transporting people or goods, there is no need to mention this in defining any particular kind of vehicle, such as a bicycle; and likewise for wheels (if 'vehicle' excludes boats, sledges and horses, as it presumably does). Each definition builds on the information in the definitions of the concepts that it mentions, provided that all the concept-names are used consistently. We shall see a particularly clear illustration of this principle in unit 13, where concepts like 'brother' and 'cousin' will be analysed in terms of simpler relations which ultimately rest on the definition of 'mother' and 'father'.

The snag with this principle is obvious. You can't define one concept until you know how to define all the other concepts that are relevant to it; and *since all concepts are related to all other concepts in one giant network, where can you start?* This may strike you as an insuperable problem, but it's not. You just have to assume that every word you use in your definitions has at least one sense, even if you don't yet know how to define that sense; and you have to try as hard as you can to avoid using any word in more than one sense. You just do the best you can, bearing in mind that you may have to come back and revise some things in the light of future work. Eveything you do is provisional, and certainty increases gradually as you cover more data. What should make it all worthwhile is the knowledge that the network is part of your mind, so however unclear the light may be, at least it's shining on you!

Having got used to the idea that word meaning is based on a network of relations among word-senses, it's time we looked more carefully at the nature of these relations. In the next unit we shall consider some very familiar concepts which are defined almost entirely in terms of relationships.

EXERCISES ✎

1 It doesn't matter what names you choose for senses but choosing names can stretch your imagination. The diagram below contains my suggestions for the senses of STAR$_n$, with a classifier for each sense as a clue to its definition:

Senses of STAR$_n$:

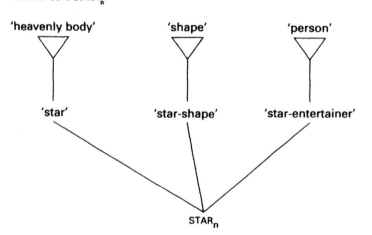

Now do the same for the lexemes in this list:

FINGER$_n$, HEAD$_n$, TOP$_n$

SEE$_v$, WORK$_v$

2 The definition for the verb CYCLE$_v$ should show explicitly that it is a hyponym of RIDE; for instance, according to *CCSD*, 'If you cycle, you ride a bicycle', where 'cycle' is shown to be equivalent to 'ride a bicycle'.

(a) Suggest definitions for the following verbs which show explicitly how they are related to other verbs in the verb-list in the appendix.

FRY, SCRIBBLE, SHUFFLE, WALTZ

(b) Check the definitions of these lexemes in a dictionary, to see if they show the relations you have identified.
(c) For each lexeme, find at least one fact about its sense which can be omitted from the definition because it is implied by the classifier.

---

3 Comment on the following definitions (from *CCSD*), which should help you to remember that dictionaries are written by mere humans:

(a) CAT:
    (i) A cat is a small, furry animal with a tail, whiskers and sharp claws. Cats are often kept as pets.
    (ii) A cat is also any larger animal that is a type of cat, such as a lion or tiger.

(b) COW_n:
    (i) A cow is a large female animal kept on farms for its milk.
    (ii) A cow is also any animal of this species, either male or female.

(c) $ROCK_n$:
    (i) Rock is the hard substance which the earth is made of.
    (ii) A rock is a piece of stone sticking out of the ground or the sea, or that has broken away from a mountain or cliff.

(d) $STONE_n$:
    (i) Stone is a hard, solid substance found in the ground and often used for building.
    (ii) A stone is a small piece of rock.

(Please remember that these examples are exceptions; most of the *CCSD* definitions are sensible, helpful and consistent!)

9 ARGUMENTS

Some concepts are defined by a **relation** between an **argument** and a **value**. If such a concept is the sense of a word, then the value is the word's referent and the argument is expressed by some accompanying word, often a possessive or one introduced by <u>of</u>.

To decide whether something is or is not a bicycle, all you need to know is the definition of 'bicycle'. If the thing has all, or most, of the characteristics described there, then it passes; if not, not. Now compare this with the sense of the lexeme ENEMY. This is quite different, because no-one is simply an enemy; you have to be an enemy of someone in particular. You may be my enemy, but someone else's friend. Whereas the range of potential referents for BICYCLE is (at least in principle) always the same, the range for ENEMY varies according to who the other person is: one range for <u>enemy of Dick</u>, another for <u>enemy of Tom</u> and yet another for <u>enemy of Harry</u>. You decide whether or not someone is my enemy by studying their relationship to me; you can't do it without including me in the equation.

The use of 'equation' in the last sentence is intended to put you into a mathematical frame of mind, because lexemes like ENEMY are like mathematical 'functions' which give different numbers according to which other number they are applied to. One function is '2 x' (multiplication by 2, or doubling), which gives 4 when applied to 2 (2 x 2), 6 when applied to 3, and so on. The same is true of the function (in this sense) 'enemy of', which yields different ranges of people (possible referents) according to whether it is applied to Tom, Dick or Harry. The term that mathematicians use for the number that a function is applied to is 'ARGUMENT', so '2 x' produces a number which is twice as great as its argument; and the number that the function produces is its 'VALUE'. Thus if the argument of '2 x' is 3, its

Argument

Value

46

value is 6, and so on. We shall use <u>argument</u> and <u>value</u> in the same way.

We have a special notation for diagramming the relation between a concept and its argument: a curved arrow pointing from the argument to the value, with the name of the relationship (e.g. 'enemy') labelling the arrow. (You can think of the arrow like a signpost saying 'This way to the . . .', where the dots stand for the label on the arrow.) If the argument is expressed by another word, as it often is, this arrow binds the meanings of the two together, so argument relations give us a chance to start analysing words in combination. The argument is always the other word's referent, so the following patterns are typical:

(1)

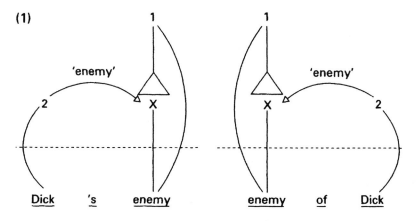

The argument doesn't have to be made explicit by other words, but if it is not it must be implicit. It is quite possible and normal to use ENEMY without naming the argument explicitly, as in (2):

> (2) When cornered he turned round to face the enemy, ready to fight.

In this example, it is clear from the context that he himself is the argument of 'enemy', so this word refers to his enemy. Nor need the argument be specific and known; it can be completely vague, or it may even be denied existence as in (3):

> (3) After all the recent unpleasantness I've decided never again to be treated as an enemy. I'd much rather be everyone's friend.

The fact remains that you can't be an enemy without an argument (in the technical sense!).

What is special about relational concepts like 'enemy' is that their definitions focus entirely on the relations between the value and the argument. It is true that the definition of 'bicycle' involved relations – and indeed, the 'network' view of knowledge means that every fact involves a relation between two concepts, so relations are fundamental to all kinds of word meaning. But each fact about 'bicycle' related it to a different other thing, as we showed in our 'bicycle-wheel' diagram of the network round 'bicycle'. In contrast, every fact in the definition of 'enemy' has to do with the relation between the same two people. These facts are something like the list in (4).

(4) If you are my enemy, then:

    a. You hate me.
    b. I hate you.
    c. You want to harm me.
    d. I want to harm you.

You may disagree about some of these facts, but whatever the details the point is that they all mention both of us. If we add them to our diagram, they need to be connected to the argument of 'enemy' as well as to the sense of ENEMY:

(5) *A definition of 'enemy'*

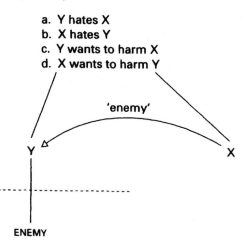

a. Y hates X
b. X hates Y
c. Y wants to harm X
d. X wants to harm Y

'enemy'

Y   X

ENEMY

The X and Y in this diagram have the same role as in an algebraic equation: each stands for anything at all, but whatever it stands for in one fact, it stands for the same thing (or person) in every other fact. In other words, they are 'variables'.

Relational senses like 'enemy' raise problems for dictionary-writers, because they are hard to define without including the argument explicitly in the definition. Here is a fairly typical attempt to define it (from the 1978 edition of the *Longman Dictionary of Contemporary English*):

(6) *ENEMY*
1. a person who hates or dislikes another person; one of 2 or more people who hate or dislike each other: *His behaviour made him many enemies* (= made many people dislike him).I *John and Paul are enemies* (= of each other).
2. someone or something that hurts, wants to harm, or is against (someone or something): *The army advanced to meet the enemy. I William Wilberforce was the enemy of slavery.*

This definition gives the impression that 'enemy' is a kind of person, namely a person who hates someone else. This kind of definition is indeed possible for a lexeme like MISANTHROPE (again from the same dictionary):

(7) *MISANTHROPE*
a person who hates everybody, trusts no one, and avoids being in the company of others.

But it doesn't work at all for ENEMY because it misses the relational basis for the definition.

This problem is solved in *CCSD* (and all the other Collins Cobuild dictionaries) by adopting a much more flexible approach to definitions. Instead of trying to find a phrase which can replace just the word being defined, it uses complete sentences in which the word being defined is accompanied by other words that refer to its argument. Here, then, is the *CCSD* definition for ENEMY.

(8) 1. You can describe someone who intends to harm you as your enemy . . . *an enemy of society.*
2. In a war, the enemy is the army or country that you are fighting . . . *the enemy had been forced back . . . enemy aircraft.*

The first part includes <u>your</u> to refer to the argument, and then repeats this argument in the definition: <u>to harm you</u>. This makes it clear that as the referent of <u>you</u> varies, so the referent of ENEMY will vary as well, which is the main requirement.

🖉 **EXERCISES**

1 We have made a fundamental distinction in this unit between two kinds of concept, relational (e.g. 'enemy') and non-relational (e.g. 'bicycle'). Which of the other nouns in the noun-list in the appendix have relational senses? (Remember: relational concepts are defined primarily in terms of the relationships between the same pair of concepts; so the fact that a bicycle normally belongs to someone is not enough in itself to make 'bicycle' a relational concept because its primary definition is in terms of facts about wheels and so on, each of which relates it to a different concept.)

---

2 The argument of one word's sense may be the referent of some accompanying word (linked to the first by <u>of</u> or <u>'s</u>). This pattern is shown in diagram (1). Suppose the argument itself is the referent of a relational concept; in this case the pattern repeats itself.

(a) Do a diagram for the semantic structure of each of the following:

(i) <u>Dick's enemy's friend</u>
(ii) <u>the enemy of the friend of Dick</u>
(iii) <u>the friend of Dick's enemy</u>

(b) Which of these phrases is ambiguous, and what are its two meanings?

(c) Assume the following situation:

Dick is Tom's friend, and Harry is Dick's enemy but Tom's friend.

Diagram their social relations using argument arrows with 'enemy' or 'friend' attached to each of the arrows.

(d) Assuming the same situation, who is a possible referent of the last word in each of the following phrases?

(i) Tom's friend
(ii) Dick's enemy
(iii) Harry's enemy
(iv) Tom's friend's enemy
(v) Dick's enemy's friend
(vi) Dick's friend's enemy
(vii) Harry's friend's friend

REVISION OF TERMINOLOGY AND CONCEPTS

This is a good moment to take stock of your tools for analysing word meanings, because the remaining units will just apply these tools without introducing new ones. Each of the units so far has introduced some kind of idea or relationship that helps in the analysis of word meaning, together with its technical terminology. The following summary is complete:

- The technical terms are:

(1) ARGUMENT, ANAPHORA, CLASSIFICATION, CLASSIFIER, DEFINITION, DISTINGUISHER, HYPONYM (CHAIN), (INFLECTIONAL) FORM, LEXEME, PROTOTYPE, REFERENT, RELATIONAL CONCEPT, SENSE, SYNONYM, VALUE, WORD-SHAPE

- The conventions for writing different kinds of 'word' are:

(2) LEXEMES, 'meanings', <u>word-shapes</u>.

- The diagramming conventions for indicating various kinds of relationships:

argument–value	curved labelled arrow pointing from the argument to the value
classification	triangle with its base on the general class and pointing, via straight lines, towards its members
referent	curved line (no arrow) from the word to its referent
sense	straight vertical or diagonal line from the word to its sense
word–meaning	horizontal broken line above words and below meanings

This notation is all illustrated in diagram (3).

(3)

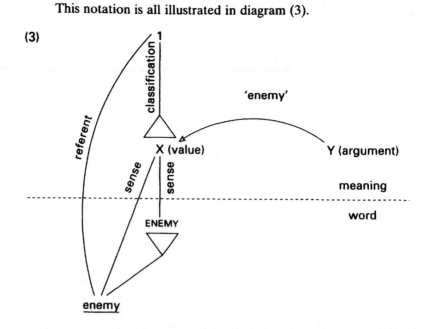

These are the tools that you will need for analysing the word meanings that we shall be exploring in the remaining units, but first we must just address one more general issue: where do the word-meaning links come from? We have already touched on this briefly in noting that the links can change through time, but the question deserves a little more attention.

CHANGE

10

> Word meanings may change through time, so an earlier meaning has no claim to be 'the true' meaning.

Why do words have the meanings they do have? Why, for instance, does FOOT mean 'foot' (rather than, say, 'cat' or 'smile')? Is there something about the sounds that make up FOOT which make this lexeme particularly suitable for conveying the sense 'foot', and no other sense? A moment's thought shows that this can't be so – FOOT has another sense as well ('foot-measure', i.e. 12 inches), and the sense 'foot' is carried in other languages by lexemes that sound quite different (French PIED, Welsh TROED, Turkish AYAK and so on). This shows that the link between a lexeme and its sense is ARBITRARY **Arbitrary** – any string of sounds can be paired with any sense. On the other hand, we can't make up the pairings as we go along, Humpty-Dumpty fashion, because successful communication demands that we use each lexeme with a sense that our hearer can guess. I use FOOT with the sense 'foot' because I know that you give it that sense, and I know this because, so far as I know, every other English speaker does the same as well. This shows that the link between lexemes and senses is CONVENTIONAL – we follow the (unwritten and often unspoken) con- **Conventional** ventions of the society in which we live.

But where do these conventions come from? More personally, how do I know that FOOT goes with 'foot'? I know because I have heard other people, including my parents, using FOOT in this way. But how did these other people know it? Same answer: because they learned it from their parents. And so on and on – through how many generations?

Well, we know that the same pairing existed in Old English (before 1066), because we have written records containing it. (The word-form is slightly different in pronunciation, but the lexeme is still the same.)

We can assume without much doubt that it existed in the language which subsequently developed into all the modern Germanic languages (German, Swedish, etc., as well as English), because similar forms are used, with the same sense, in all these languages (German FUSS, Swedish FOT – all the variations in form can be explained and have nothing to do with the sense). Historians call this ancestor language Proto-Germanic, and date it to about 2000 BC. But the same kind of detective work brings in data from other language groups and allows the date to be pushed even further back. In Latin the lexeme derived from the same ancestor as our FOOT was PED- (to which various suffixes were added; compare our words derived from Latin such as PEDESTRIAN), and in Greek it was POD- (think of TRI-POD); but the language that developed into these two plus Proto-Germanic (among others) was Proto-Indoeuropean, which was probably spoken about 4000 BC or earlier.

The outcome of all this detective work is that we can trace the FOOT–'foot' link which I learned from my parents through an unbroken chain of learners spanning at least 6,000 years. At four generations per century, that makes 240 generations, which is impressive (even astonishing) as an example of consistency in cultural transmission, especially when we consider that it has worked in exactly the same way for every other native speaker of English, of whom there must be at least 300 million alive today. More impressively still, it's not just English that continues this long tradition. A German speaker who links 'foot' to FUSS and a French speaker who links it to PIED are in fact part of exactly the same tradition, which probably brings the number of living adherents nearer to 1,000 million – a quite amazing example of cultural continuity.

However, this isn't the whole picture. For every lexeme that still has the same sense as it did in Proto-Indoeuropean there are hundreds that don't. For one thing, the sense of a lexeme can shift gradually, just as its word-form can. Take BEAR$_v$, as in (3).

> (3) a. She bore the pain bravely.
>   b. Our old apple tree didn't bear any fruit this year.
>   c. They bore him on a stretcher.

This is descended from a Proto-Indoeuropean lexeme meaning 'carry', and all the meanings illustrated in (3) are clearly related to this sense. Indeed, the one in (3c) is simply 'carry', but the style is archaic or formal. The fact is that this is no longer the ordinary lexeme for 'carry'. At various points in its history, the transmission of senses from generation to generation has been imperfect.

Another major source of change is the invention of new lexemes. This is happening all the time nowadays, and it has always been common. Most new lexemes are based on existing lexemes with more or less relevant senses; for example, BEARABLE is based on BEAR$_v$, but only uses the 'tolerate' sense. What makes the picture really complicated is that very often the model lexemes are in other languages, but are cousins to existing lexemes. An example is

PEDAL, which used to mean 'treadle' when it was borrowed from French PÉDALE about 400 years ago; French borrowed it from Italian PEDALE, which got it from Latin PEDAL- meaning 'of the foot'. In Latin PEDAL- is based on PED-, 'foot' – which, as we have just seen, is directly descended from the same Proto-Indoeuropean lexeme as English FOOT! So there is a historical link between our lexemes FOOT and PEDAL, though a complicated one. A similar link can be found between English BEAR$_v$ and a host of lexemes containing -FER- (TRANSFER, PREFER, REFER, DIFFER, DIFFERENT and so on), all of which are descended from a Latin lexeme FER- which meant 'carry' and which in turn was directly descended from the same Proto-Indoeuropean lexeme as English BEAR$_v$. (Another related lexeme is the Greek PHOR-, again meaning 'carry', which occurs in our technical term ANA-PHORA and relates it to the Latin RE-FER, as we saw in **Unit 2**.)

The examples illustrate gradual shifts of meaning, but cumulatively these shifts can result in dramatic changes. My favourite example is TREACLE, which can be traced back to the classical Greek THER-, 'wild animal'! (THERI-, 'small wild animal' > THERIAK-, 'of a small wild animal' > 'antidote against a poisonous bite' (medieval French) > medieval English TRIACLE, 'medicinal compound used as antidote to poison' > modern English TREACLE, 'treacle'.) For good measure, it is possible that TREACLE is related via THER- to FIERCE, DEER and DEITY!

So where do the conventions of modern English come from? Some of them are directly inherited from previous generations as far back as we can trace; but some – probably the majority – are not. It is very easy to see that conventions can change, because we can see changes happening in front of our eyes (or ears). Every generation introduces its share of changes, and in my lifetime many lexemes have changed their senses – acquired new senses, lost old ones, or shifted definitions. MOUSE has acquired 'mouse-computer', JOLLY has lost 'very' (e.g. jolly good), GAY has acquired 'homosexual' and lost 'merry', and the definition of 'nurse' has become sex-neutral.

This discussion of change leaves us with two important conclusions. The first is that if meanings change, the only facts that are relevant to current meanings are facts about current usage. Earlier uses of a lexeme may be interesting, even fascinating, but in general they are interesting precisely because they are *different* from modern usage. There is no point in bewailing changes as though some earlier state of 'correct' usage was being lost, and it is silly to use earlier meanings as evidence in an argument about the 'real' meaning of a word; e.g. the fact that SCIENCE used to mean simply 'knowledge' is irrelevant to its modern sense.

The second conclusion is that the conventions may be less uniformly accepted than we think, especially when it comes to the finer details of definitions. Is a tricycle a kind of bicycle? Does a 16-year-old in school count as a student? Are you climbing if you go from the street up onto the pavement? When I ask questions like these in class, my students usually disagree among themselves. There is no need to argue about who is 'right'. This is the wrong question to ask, because your task is to explore your *own* system, even if it turns out that you are the only person in the world who has that particular system. Of course, if you do discover that you are out of step with the rest of the world, you may decide to change your usage; but that is a different matter.

The next unit will focus on one small but important area of your system, the part that deals with the major classification of the world into human and non-human. You may find differences between yourself and other people even in this fundamental area of meaning.

EXERCISES ✎

1 English is changing before our eyes.

    (a) The following lexemes have changed their meanings in the last few decades. How, and why?

        CRACK, GIG, GO (think what you can say after 'He went ...'), GREEN, WELL, WICKED

    (b) Find two other examples of lexemes that have changed recently.

2 One way in which meanings can change is called 'contraction', in which the range of possible referents contracts; and the opposite direction of change is called 'generalisation'. For example, HOUND used to mean 'dog', but this meaning has now contracted to 'hunting-dog'; and meanwhile DOG has generalised from 'dog of a particular (ancient) breed' to any 'dog'!

    (a) Decide whether the senses of the following lexemes have contracted or generalised in relation to the earlier senses that are shown on the right.

AFFECTION	'feeling'
BIRD	'young birdling'
DEER	'animal'
FOWL	'bird'
MEAT	'food'
PIG	'young pig'
PLACE	'town square'
STARVE	'die'
UNDERTAKER	'contractor'
VIRTUE	'manliness'
WIFE	'woman'

    (b) Give a general definition of these two kinds of change in terms of classification and classifiers, such as 'When a lexeme's sense generalises, the classifier of its sense ...'

3 Pick out any words in the following Shakespeare quotations which have meanings that are now defunct, and try to define these meanings.

(a) Let's have one other gaudy night. (*Antony and Cleopatra*)

(b) He that wants money, means and content is without three good things. (*As You Like It*)

(c) It is meat and drink to me to see a clown. (*As You Like It*)

(d) Bid them wash their faces and keep their teeth clean. (*Coriolanus*)

(e) All is not well; I doubt some foul play. (*Hamlet*)

11 HUMANITY

> A study of word meaning shows that we make a fundamental distinction between humans and the rest of the world, which conflicts with the classification of humans as animals.

Suppose you were asked to group the following 'entities' into two classes, what would you do?

    (1) a. a man
          b. a cow
          c. a rock

Would you group the cow with the man or with the rock? This is a rather artificial activity so you may have no clear answer. After all, you could argue for either grouping according to whether you are considering the division between living and non-living (cow = man) or the one between human and non-human (cow = rock). However English forces us to make similar decisions dozens of times each day, and any speaker of English gives a consistent answer: the cow goes with the rock, not with the man.

One situation where English forces the question is in choosing an 'interrogative pronoun' – a question word beginning with *wh*-. Do you use WHAT or WHO? If the answer could be a man, you use WHO, but if it could be a cow or a rock, it has to be WHAT. Imagine yourself looking at a scene with a friend, and saying one of the following:

    (2) a. Who's that over there?
          b. What's that over there?

If you're sure that the answer must be a human you have to use (2a), and it's equally obligatory to use (2b) if you're sure it's not a human. What if you don't know either way? In that case you presumably use

(2b), but it's not a completely satisfactory solution. If your friend knows that it's (for example) your daughter, then she might tease you for mistaking your daughter for a (mere) thing.

Does English provide any way to avoid the choice? No, it doesn't; nor does it contain a satisfactory general noun which can apply equally well to humans and non-humans, which is why I had to use the philosopher's term ENTITY in quotes in the first sentence of this unit. To convince yourself that this is not in fact a satisfactory solution, imagine yourself using this word to a friend in a sentence like (3)!

(3) Which of those two entities over there do you think is my daughter?

It is often claimed that every language is perfectly suited to the needs of its speakers. This is just not so; we English speakers sometimes need to be able to refer to 'entities' without defining their humanity, but the language fails us. This is one example among many of language as a rather limited medium for expressing our ideas, to balance the equally true view of language as a lifeline to communication and complex thought. I am not of course suggesting that the lack of a proper, ordinary, word for 'entity' stops us from entertaining this concept; on the contrary, it is precisely because we do entertain it that we want to be able to communicate it, and run into trouble.

The choice between interrogative WHO and WHAT is not the only place where English forces the choice between human and non-human upon us. Here is a list of other pairs:

(4)

Human	Non-human
WHO (Who are you looking at?)	WHAT (What are you looking at?)
WHO (the girl who I married)	WHICH (the cow which I bought)
SOMEONE	SOMETHING
ANYONE	ANYTHING
NO-ONE	NOTHING
EVERYONE	EVERYTHING
HE, SHE, ONE	IT
PERSON	THING

As you can see, most of these lexemes are very commonly used, and at a very conservative guess we probably choose from this list hundreds of times every day in speaking or writing, to say nothing of the times when we hear others using them. Every time we do so the choice between human and non-human is forced upon us; and in most cases there is no way to avoid the choice by picking a more general term, for the simple reason that there is no more general term. (There are exceptions: for example, the choice between WHO and WHICH can be avoided by using THAT: *the girl that I married* and *the cow that I bought.*)

How clear are the concepts 'person' and 'thing'? On the whole, the first is very clear, though it is in practice unclear at what point a foetus turns into a person, and it is worth noticing that even babies are often referred to by IT. The concept 'thing' is much less clear; e.g. is London a thing? And what about the number 3? The typical thing is a discrete concrete object, but other 'things' may be treated as 'honorary things' for lack of a better cover term. The need for such a term arises in sentences like (5):

(5) In this department we teach things like syntax, semantics and phonetics.

On the other hand, I should be reluctant to describe semantics as a difficult thing - a difficult subject maybe, but not a difficult thing. It is interesting to notice that the concept 'person' has been part of English word meaning for thousands of years, although it has jumped from lexeme to lexeme in that time. In Old English it belonged to the (ancestor of our) lexeme MAN, and the sense 'man' belonged to WER (as in WEREWOLF and more distantly VIRILE and VIRTUE!). Then 'person' transferred to PERSON (borrowed from French), and 'man' shifted to MAN. These changes are shown in the diagram, which shows how the links between lexemes and senses can change without necessarily affecting those between one sense and another.

(6)   Old English   Modern English

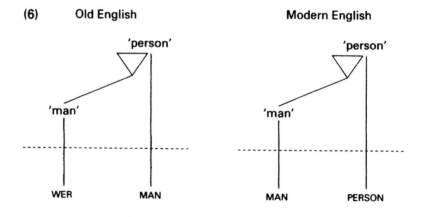

The history of THING is much messier, as it derives from an Old English word which also meant a collection of people!

The evidence so far seems to point very strongly to a major division in our minds between people and everything else. But there is a problem. We've already looked at a lexeme which is highly relevant in this context, ANIMAL. You may remember that this was one of our main examples in **Unit 8**, where we noted that it has two senses which we called 'animal' and 'non-plant'. We quoted a dictionary definition for the 'non-plant' sense:

(7) 2 An animal is also any living thing that is not a plant, including people.

Note the 'including people': a person is an animal, which is a thing. Can this be right, as a statement about how we use ANIMAL? The kind of example that lies behind the definition is illustrated by (8):

(8) a. **Man is a very weak animal.**

b. **It is this that divides us from the rest of the animal kingdom.**

These examples do seem to prove the point: we do sometimes use ANIMAL to include people.

Where does this leave the whole of our earlier discussion? It would seem that we are operating (at least) two different, and competing, semantic systems at the same time. On the one hand we have the PERSON–THING system, in which cows fall together with rocks but not with people, and on the other we have the system implied by the 'non-plant' sense of ANIMAL, where cows are grouped with humans in contrast with rocks (and trees). These go with two quite distinct views of the world, but somehow we manage to accommodate them both in our minds.

How do we get away with it? Presumably the answer is fairly clear: we apply different classifications according to immediate purposes, according to whether we are engaged in ordinary everyday life or in science. Even scientists operate the PERSON–THING system as citizens, whatever they do as scientists. The message for science is rather dismal: after a century of Darwinian evolution, the idea that people are fundamentally different from animals is still very strong thanks to the backing it receives from various sources, of which perhaps the most influential is our language.

We can summarise these conclusions by the following diagram of classification relations, in which the dotted line shows the scientific classification.

(9)

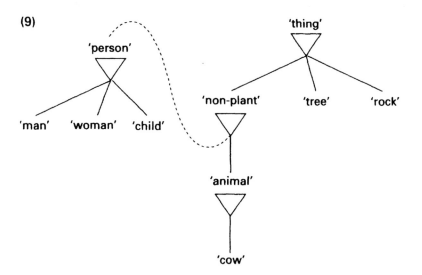

EXERCISES ✎

1 One of the reasons why the concept 'person' plays such an important part in English vocabulary is that we know so many facts about
people - i.e. all the things that are true of any typical person, and not
just of some individual or group of people. Here are two such facts:

(i) A person has a name.
(ii) A person wears clothes.

(a) Give five more facts, of as different types as possible (e.g.
not all to do with parts of our bodies).

(b) What you believe to be true of the typical person depends,
of course, on your experiences, which depends on the
society in which you live. Think of one fact which a member of some other society is likely to consider typically
human but which you don't (or vice versa).

(c) Small babies are not typical humans. List two respects in
which they are exceptional.

(d) Think of one belief about typical humans which you know
is widely accepted but which you think is false and deserves
to be called a prejudice.

---

2 Use the noun-list in the appendix as a source of examples.

(a) Find ten nouns that can only be used to refer to people.

(b) Find ten that can only be used to refer to things.

(c) Are there any that can be used, with the same sense, to
refer either to a person or to a thing?

---

3 We have distinct names for wholes and parts – e.g. BICYCLE and
WHEEL – but the whole and its parts may be classified differently in
terms of their humanity. (You can test the classification by using a
pronoun to refer to the 'thing' concerned: your choice between IT
and SHE or HE gives the answer.)

(a) Are parts of people people? Find at least one example in
the noun-list in the appendix of a person-part which is not
a person.

(b) Can people be parts of things? Find at least one example of
a thing whose parts are people.

PARENTS

> The senses of MOTHER and FATHER are defined by a large number of facts, with a great deal of variation which reflects current social changes. The sense of PARENT may be nothing more than 'mother or father of X'.

In this unit we shall apply our tools to a more complicated pair of concepts, 'mother' and 'father'. Two facts about these concepts make them more complicated than 'person'. The first fact is that they are relational – i.e. they are like 'enemy' rather than 'bicycle'. Each one defines one person (the mother or father) in terms of their relationship to another person (the child), so in the case of 'mother' the mother is the value and the child is the argument. The diagram for the sense of MOTHER is as in (1), where Y could be the referent of a possessive such as <u>my</u>:

(1)

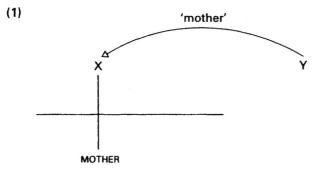

The second fact is that 'mother' and 'father' are excellent examples of prototypes, defined only in terms of clear cases rather than in terms of watertight boundaries. Let's start with 'mother'. Let's assume an adult called Mary and a child called Charlie. In the simple case, the following facts (along with several others) will be true of the relation between Mary and Charlie:

(2) a. Mary conceived Charlie – i.e. she supplied both the egg which eventually turned into Charlie, and the uterus in which the egg was fertilised.
    b. Mary bore Charlie.
    c. Mary 'nurtures' (or nurtured) Charlie – i.e. she has played a major role in caring for him until he was big enough to look after himself.

If all these facts are true, Mary is quite definitely and indisputably Charlie's mother. If you're unsure about any of these facts, you can apply the <u>but</u> and <u>so</u> tests. It should be possible to start with <u>Mary</u> is <u>Charlie's</u> <u>mother</u>, <u>so . . .</u>, and to continue with any of a–c; or to start with <u>Mary</u> is <u>Charlie's</u> <u>mother</u>, <u>but . .</u> , continuing with a denial of any of a–c (e.g. . . . but she didn't conceive him).

The problem is that the world is sufficiently complex for these facts to be independent of one another (even if only to a limited extent), which allows mismatches to arise; for example, it is common for a child conceived and born by one woman to be nurtured by another. If this is true of Mary and Charlie, then she is his mother in some respects, but not in all. Modern surgery even allows one woman's egg to be inserted into another woman's uterus, which complicates the picture further.

Some untypical cases are anticipated by our vocabulary, because they arise sufficiently frequently to justify a special category. We have terms like ADOPTIVE and BIRTH (or BIOLOGICAL) which can be combined with MOTHER to define the common mismatch situations. But there will always be some situations that arise too rarely to merit a special label. Suppose, for instance, that Mary gives Charlie up for adoption because she can't care for him, but that the adoptive parents are killed in an accident, leaving Charlie an 'orphan' (or is he?). By now Mary has matured to the extent of being capable of caring for him herself; in order to get back her parental rights she has to adopt him back, so she is then both his adoptive mother and his birth mother. We have no term to cover this case, and she is certainly not a typical mother.

The next diagram summarises the partial definition of 'mother' given above. As with the definition of 'enemy' in unit 9, all the facts involve both the mother and the argument, called 'Y'.

(3)

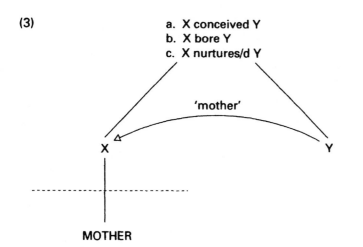

a. X conceived Y
b. X bore Y
c. X nurtures/d Y

'mother'

X

Y

MOTHER

The definition of 'father' presumably follows similar lines, but you can work it out for yourself in the exercises.

Our analysis so far misses rather an obvious fact about mothers and fathers: mothers are female and fathers are male. (Once again we're talking prototypes, though exceptions are harder to imagine in this case; how about the effects of sex-change operations?) It is easy to build the sex contrast into our analysis, because it is another relational concept. Everybody has a sex, just as everybody has a mother. Admittedly your sex is an abstraction ('male' or 'female') whereas your mother is a person, but we can use the same diagramming techniques for linking the argument to its value on the sex contrast. Here is a more complete diagram for 'mother'.

(4)

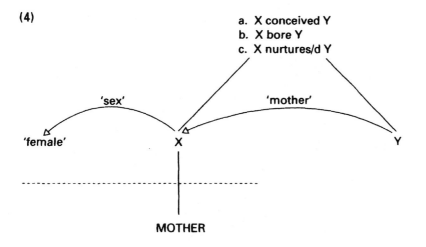

a. X conceived Y
b. X bore Y
c. X nurtures/d Y

'sex'   'mother'

'female'   X   Y

MOTHER

Every other female concept shares the same 'female' value, so this arrow links 'mother' almost directly to other concepts like 'sister', 'woman' and 'lioness'.

Mothers and fathers are all parents. What is the definition of 'parent'? The answer is much less obvious than you may think, and may vary from person to person. It all depends on whether you think mothers and fathers have anything in common, by being mothers and fathers. There are some obvious differences – the mother gives birth to the child, but the father doesn't – so we can be sure that 'mother' means more than 'female parent', with all the defining characteristics attached to 'parent' rather than to 'mother'.

Granted that there are differences between mothers and fathers, are there any similarities? One answer is that they both nurture the child (in typical situations, remember). If this is your answer, then you could define 'parent' as follows:

(5) *PARENT*
    If X is Y's parent, then X nurtures Y through childhood.

But if this is so, it will be possible to imagine situations in which Mary is Charlie's mother without being his parent, namely if she gave birth to him but didn't nurture him. If you accept this consequence, then (5) is your definition for 'parent'. You can use 'parent' as the classifier for 'mother' and 'father', and remove all mention of nurturing from the definition of 'mother'. Diagram (6) shows what you mean by MOTHER, FATHER and PARENT:

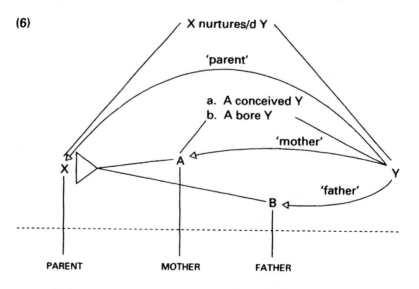

If on the other hand you think the roles of mothers and fathers are completely different, then you have a much simpler definition.

(7) *PARENT*
    X is the parent of Y if X is the mother or father of Y.

This leaves the definitions of 'mother' and 'father' unchanged, and means that anyone who qualifies as someone else's mother must automatically qualify as their parent as well.

(8)

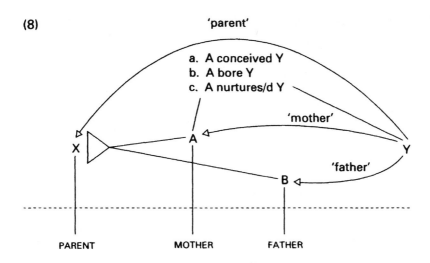

Different people seem to answer these questions in different ways, which may reflect basic differences in their view of parenthood. You will no doubt want to decide where you stand. But this discussion is important for another reason as well. For those of us who tie parenthood directly to motherhood or fatherhood, as per definition (7), the definition of 'parent' is very 'poor', and rests entirely on the 'rich' definitions of 'mother' and 'father'. In the next unit we shall see even clearer examples of this pattern, and we shall find, in fact, that all our vocabulary for family relations is more or less poor with the exception of 'mother' and 'father', which are the foundations on which the whole system rests.

✐ **EXERCISES**

1 The definition of 'mother' given in (1) is incomplete.

    (a) Add one more fact which you think is true of typical mothers.

    (b) Suggest at least two facts to be included in the definition of 'father'.

    (c) Decide whether (5) or (7) is your definition of 'parent'.

    (d) Do a diagram showing the relations among 'mother', 'father' and 'parent', taking account of your answers to the earlier questions.

    (e) Comment on the following definitions:

> MOTHER: Your mother is the woman who gave birth to you.
> FATHER: Your father is your male parent.
> PARENT: Your parents are your father and mother.

2   The following words or phrases contain MOTHER:

> ADOPTIVE MOTHER, BIRTH MOTHER, FOSTER MOTHER, GOD-MOTHER, STEP-MOTHER, MOTHER-IN-LAW

What do they mean?

---

3 Some lexemes for different-sex concepts are neatly paired off, and have a sex-neutral equivalent.

(a) Complete the following table:

Female	Male	Sex-neutral
WOMAN	MAN	PERSON
MOTHER		PARENT
DAUGHTER	SON	
	HUSBAND	SPOUSE
QUEEN		
	RAM	
		HORSE

(b) Draw a single diagram which contains all these concepts and shows their links. For example, show the similarity between 'woman' and 'mother', and also the link of 'woman' and 'man' to 'person'. Remember to show 'sex' as a relation with 'male' or 'female' as its value.

FAMILIES

13

The remaining **kinship terms**, names for one's relatives, can be defined in terms of the basic ones, MOTHER and FATHER, though extra facts are also added to the definitions.

Having defined 'mother', 'father' and 'parent', we are well placed to define the rest of English 'kinship terminology', i.e. all the lexemes used for referring to one's 'blood' relatives. The table contains a complete list (ignoring synonyms like AUNTIE and MUM, and also the open-ended possibilities allowed by adding GREAT- before GRAND-):

Female	Male	Sex-neutral
MOTHER	FATHER	PARENT
DAUGHTER	SON	CHILD
SISTER	BROTHER	(SIBLING)
GRANDMOTHER	GRANDFATHER	GRANDPARENT
GRAND- DAUGHTER	GRANDSON	GRANDCHILD
AUNT	UNCLE	
NIECE	NEPHEW	
		COUSIN

We shall see in this unit that it is possible to define the senses of all these lexemes in terms of other senses which ultimately rest on 'mother' and 'father', plus 'sex'.

Take GRANDMOTHER. Your grandmother is the mother of one of your parents, so we can define 'grandmother' in terms of 'mother' and 'parent'. It is easy to diagram this.

(1)

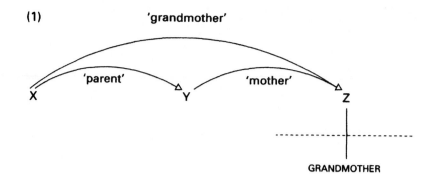

In words, (1) says that X's parent's mother is X's grandmother. This isn't of course all that we can say about grandmothers – no doubt we all know other facts about typical grandmothers, but our definition of 'grandmother' must contain *at least* the information in this diagram.

How seriously should we take the terms 'parent' and 'mother' in this diagram? Are they really the same categories that we defined in the last unit? If 'mother' really means the same here as it did in our definition of the sense of MOTHER, then the facts that we collected for MOTHER should also apply here. For example, if your mother is the person who gave birth to you, then your grandmother should also be the person who gave birth to one of your parents. Typically, this is of course true. But even more crucially, the kinds of *uncertainties* that we met with MOTHER should apply here too. If you're uncertain about whether Mary is Charlie's mother, then you should be equally uncertain about whether she is the grandmother of Charlie's children. This does seem to be the case. In other words, it is precisely the same concept 'mother' that is involved in the sense of MOTHER and of GRANDMOTHER; and it is easy to see that the same is true for 'parent'. The principle of consistency (**Unit 8**) requires us to use the same name for any given concept, so it isn't just a convenience when we build 'mother' and 'parent' into our definition of 'grandmother'; it is absolutely essential to do so.

We found in the last unit that we can't define 'mother' or 'father' as simply 'female/male parent', so the same conclusion applies to 'grandmother' and 'grandfather'. These must each be defined directly, but they can be united by 'grandparent', as the next diagram shows.

In words, X's grandmother and grandfather are X's parent's mother and father. Notice that the sex distinction applies to the grandparents, and not to the linking category, the parents. In other words, English makes no linguistic distinction between maternal and paternal grandparents. You'll see later that this is covered by a very simple generalisation about English kinship terminology.

Most of the other terms can be defined in similar ways, but DAUGHTER, SON and CHILD are different. This is because 'child' is the same relationship as 'parent', but seen from the other end; so

(2)

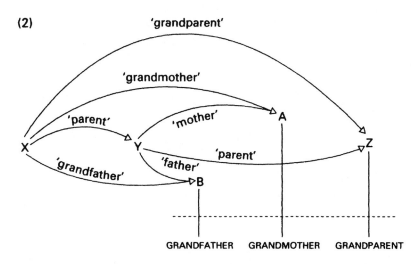

your child is someone to whom you are a parent. We can diagram this as well, but in this case we have to have two concepts connected by arrows going in both directions:

(3)

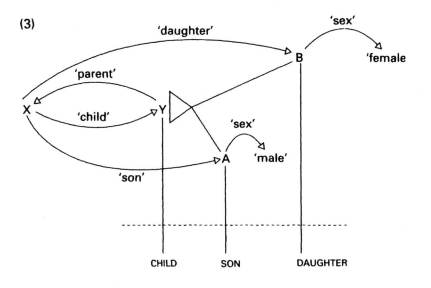

It is hard to put this into words, but one pithy attempt is: 'X's child's parent is X' – or again, 'Your child is anyone whose parent is you'. Once again you will notice that the sex attribute applies to the child, and not to the parent; that is, we don't have distinct lexemes for the child of a mother and the child of a man, though this arrangement is easy to imagine – e.g. I might be my mother's 'mon', but my father's 'fon'.

The main point of this unit has been to show how relatively distant relationships can be derived from relatively close ones by combining them in pairs. The more distant the relationship, the more abstract it becomes, but of course the values and arguments of these abstract relationships are completely concrete people like you and me. In the next unit we shall finish the course by considering a different kind of abstract concept which applies to concrete arguments.

EXERCISES ✎

1 Produce diagrams for the senses of the following groups of lexemes, and comment on any gaps in our vocabulary (i.e. concepts that have no lexeme) that you notice. Take X as the argument, as in my diagrams, and make sure you build on the definitions that we have already produced; e.g. in defining 'grandchild', make sure you exploit our definition of 'child'.

    (a) GRANDCHILD, GRANDDAUGHTER, GRANDSON
    (b) BROTHER, SISTER (Hint: assume that X can't be their own relative – e.g. I'm not my own brother!)
    (c) NEPHEW, NIECE
    (d) AUNT, UNCLE (keep to 'blood' relationships!)
    (e) COUSIN

2 I said that there is a simple generalisation about the role of sex in English kinship terminology.

    (a) What is it?
    (b) Does it apply to Latin? The following are the Latin translations for AUNT and UNCLE.

MATERTERA	'maternal aunt'
AMITA	'paternal aunt'
AVUNCULUS	'maternal uncle'
PATRUUS	'paternal uncle'

    (c) Do you know any other languages to which the English generalisation doesn't apply?

3 These terms are all hyponyms of RELATIVE$_n$, but are there different types of relative (i.e. does RELATIVE$_n$ have more than one sense)?

    (a) Which kinship terms can combine with -in-law? What's odd about AUNT and UNCLE?
    (b) Which can combine with step-?
    (c) What do these facts tell us about RELATIVE$_n$?
    (d) Suggest a definition of the relevant sense of FAMILY: 'X's family consists of . . .'.

VERBS

14

> The same kind of analysis can be applied to the meanings of verbs.

What can we say about the meaning of the verb <u>danced</u> in sentence (1)?

> (1) John danced.

Is this the same kind of meaning as the meanings we have looked at so far (and which have all been the meanings of nouns, as you have probably noticed)? The aim of this unit is to show that it is almost the same, though there will be a slight extra complication (which has nothing to do with the fact that the meanings belong to verbs rather than to nouns). In particular we shall see that we can give <u>danced</u> a sense and a referent, which are related in the usual way; we can define the sense in terms of a classifier and some distinguishers; we can find it some hyponyms; and most importantly of all, we can give it an argument. This is where the extra complication arises.

What kind of thing does <u>danced</u> refer to? We know that <u>John</u> refers to the person John, but I hope it's obvious that <u>danced</u> must be different. At least in the technical sense of REFER, <u>danced</u> can't refer to John; it doesn't pick out the person, but his action. This is a bit like separating the Cheshire Cat from its grin, but it is something we are doing all the time – in fact, every time we use a verb. Of course you can't have dancing without a dancer, though John still exists even when he's stopped dancing; but even though the referents of <u>John</u> and <u>danced</u> are unevenly matched, they are still separate.

One further piece of evidence for the referent of <u>danced</u> is that it passes the test for referents, as we saw in **Unit 2**. The evidence consists in showing that <u>it</u> can be anaphoric to <u>danced</u> as in (2):

> (2) John danced. It surprised everyone.

It shares the referent of some earlier word, which can't be <u>John</u> (which needs <u>he</u>, not <u>it</u>) and therefore must be <u>danced</u>. Another indication that <u>danced</u> has a referent just like that of a noun is that the noun DANCE$_n$ can be used to refer to the same scene:

(3) John danced. . . . John's dance surprised everyone.

Like any other noun, the word <u>dance</u> has a referent, which is an act of dancing, so why can't we say that this very same act of dancing is also the referent of <u>danced</u>?

The noun DANCE$_n$ also shows that DANCE$_v$ must have a sense. Here's how the argument runs: we assume that DANCE$_n$ has a sense, then we observe that every possible referent of DANCE$_n$ is also a possible referent of DANCE$_v$ – I at least can't imagine any situation where an action is taking place which could be referred to by the noun but not by the verb, or vice versa. This conclusion suggests that DANCE$_n$ and DANCE$_v$ both have senses, and more precisely that they have the same sense – i.e. they are synonyms! Let's call their shared sense 'dancing'. The story so far is summarised in (4), which shows the relationship between <u>danced</u> and <u>dance</u> in sentence (3).

(4)

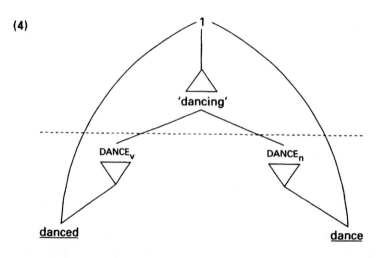

Let's try to define 'dancing'. Here is one dictionary definition (take as usual from the *Collins Cobuild Student's Dictionary*):

(5) When you dance, you move around in time to music.

According to this the classifier is 'moving' and the distinguishers are whatever <u>around</u> means and 'in time to music'. 'Dancing', then, is a special kind of 'moving'. We can certainly agree, I think, that if you aren't moving at all you aren't dancing, and that music has to be involved (via its rhythm – hence 'in time to'). The point of <u>around</u> is presumably that your whole body is involved. If my little finger moves, then you could say that I have moved; this may be what a photographer or a masked gunman wants to prevent when he says <u>Don't move!</u>, but it's not enough to qualify as dancing. We can't take the analysis much further here, so let's recognise the existence of unspecified links from 'dancing' to 'whole body' and 'musical rhythm'.

(6)

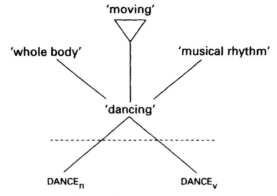

It is easy to find hyponyms of 'dancing': for instance 'waltzing', 'jiving' and 'moshing'. Interestingly, and perhaps surprisingly, a lot of the hyponyms are provided by nouns which have no corresponding verb; for instance, BALLET and ROCK-N-ROLL (which supports the claim that verbs and nouns have the same kinds of sense).

What is the relation between the dancing and John? What <u>danced</u> refers to is not dancing in general, nor any old example of dancing, but specifically dancing in which the dancer was John. As we have seen, there can't be dancing without a dancer, which reminds us of concepts like 'enemy' and 'mother' – you can't be an enemy without being an enemy of someone. In other words, 'dancing' is a relational concept, so we need a label for the relationship. Let's call it (rather unadventurously!) 'dancer'. But 'dancer' can't be the sense of DANCE because it presumably has to be used as the sense of DANCER, which is obviously not a synonym of DANCE. DANCER is used to refer to the person, while DANCE (verb or noun) refers to the action:

(7) a. The dance/!dancer was a waltz.
    b. The dancer/!dance was John.

We can see, therefore, that 'dancing' is not a relational concept of the same kind as 'enemy' or 'mother'. The difference is that it is a relation between two quite different kinds of concept – between John and his dancing. Its sense has to define the action concept in relation to other kinds of actions, music and so on (rather like the definition of 'bicycle'), but it also involves the relationship to the dancer as an essential ingredient. In other words, a concept such as 'dancing' is a complicated blend of the characteristics of relational and non-relational concepts. We can see that the diagram for 'dancing' in (6) is quite incomplete, so here is a better attempt:

(8)

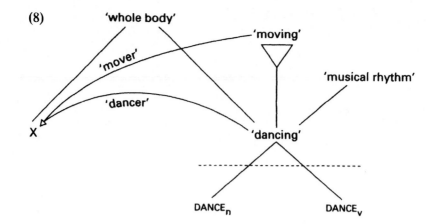

I have added arrows showing that 'X' is the dancer and also the mover, and the extra line between X and 'whole body' is meant to show that it is X's whole body that moves.

Another way of describing the concept 'dancing' is to say that it is a non-relational concept whose definition involves a relational concept. Thus 'dancing' is the label for a meeting-point in the network of arrows, and is different from the label 'dancer' on the arrow joining it to the person concerned. As soon as you see it like this, you can see another potential complication on the horizon: that a concept could involve more than one relationship.

For examples of this you don't have to look for very complicated concepts. Take 'eating' for instance:

(9) John ate a biscuit.

Eating cannot take place unless there is not only an eater, but also some food. The definition of 'eating' has to involve both, as in the following (from *CCSD*):

(10) When you eat something, you put it into your mouth, chew it and swallow it.

Notice how each of the three parts of the definition involves both 'you' (the eater) and 'it' (the food). 'Eating', then, is a two-argument concept.

This definition is a suitable point to end the course because it hints at some forbidding complexities in word meaning. If there can be two arguments, why not three or more? (Why not indeed? Think of I lent you my bicycle or I sold you my bicycle for twenty pounds.) Where has the classifier gone? (Maybe 'eating' is also a kind of 'affecting', so (10) is only part of the definition?) The three stages of eating have to take place in the order given; how does that kind of organisation fit into our theory of definitions? (Think of the difference between reaching London and leaving London; in both cases there is one stage where you are in London, and another where you are not, but the order is different.) If 'eating' can be defined in terms of 'putting', 'chewing' and 'swallowing', these concepts are presumably simpler

(11)

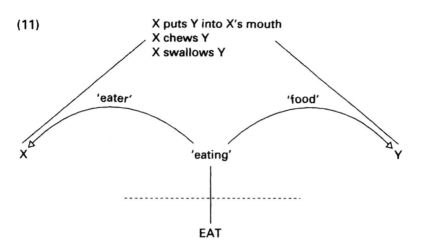

X puts Y into X's mouth
X chews Y
X swallows Y

'eater'   'food'

X   'eating'   Y

EAT

than 'eating'; so can we break down 'putting' and so on into simpler concepts, and go on splitting until we reach . . . what? Is it turtles all the way down?[1]

📝 **EXERCISES**

1 Each of the following *CCSD* definitions belongs to one sense of one of the words in the verb-list in the appendix. Guess the verbs concerned, and if you have a copy of *CCSD*, check your answers. How good do you think these definitions are?

(a) When you . . . something that is written down, you look at written words or symbols and understand them.
(b) If you . . . something, you find it pleasant or attractive, or you approve of it.
(c) When you . . . something, you try using it in order to find out what it is, what condition it is in, or how well it works.
(d) If you . . . someone or something, you look at them for a period of time, and pay attention to what is happening.
(e) When you . . . something, you carry or support it, usually using your fingers or your arms.

---

2 DANCE_n and DANCE_v are synonyms because they share a sense, 'dancing'; but they also share a word-shape, <u>dance</u>, so to that extent they are 'homonyms' as well. In contrast, the noun that is synonymous with ARRIVE is ARRIVAL, which is not a homonym.

(a) Find five other examples in the verb-list which are both synonyms and homonyms of nouns.
(b) Find two examples in the verb-list which have noun synonyms which are not homonyms.

[1]There is a famous story which I have seen in various forms, but which always involves someone claiming that the world is sitting on the back of a giant turtle; and when asked what holds the turtle up, they say triumphantly that 'it's turtles all the way down'.

(c) Find two examples in the verb-list which have noun homonyms which are not synonyms.

---

3 The person who dances is the dancer, and the one who eats is the eater. DANCER and EATER are formed in a regular way by adding -ER to the verb, so let's call them 'regular do-er nouns'. Not all nouns ending in -ER are regular do-er nouns (think of MOTHER!), and not all do-er nouns end in -ER (think of RECIPIENT).

(a) Find three verbs in the verb-list for which there is a regular do-er noun like DANCER.

(b) Find one verb which has an -ER noun which refers to an 'instrument', i.e. the relevant tool or machine, rather than to the person who does the action.

(c) Now change lists, to the noun-list. Find three nouns that are regular do-er nouns like DANCER.

(d) Find three nouns that end in -ER or -OR without being do-er nouns.

(e) Find three do-er nouns with irregular forms (e.g. someone who accompanies you on the piano is an accompanist, not an accompanier).

(f) Find three do-er nouns with irregular meanings – i.e. which consist of some verb plus -ER or -OR, but whose sense isn't what you'd expect.

---

4 Eating is an important part of our lives, so the vocabulary for talking about it is rich and highly interconnected; but there are some surprising gaps.

(a) Suggest a definition of 'food'.

(b) Define 'chew', 'munch', 'bite' and 'gnaw'.

(c) Define 'drinking', the sense of DRINK$_v$.

(d) Do a diagram for 'drinking' like the one for 'eating'.

(e) Is the sense of the noun DRINK$_n$ similar to 'food' or to 'eating'?

(f) Is there an ordinary verb that covers both eating and drinking?

(g) Is there an ordinary noun that covers both food and drink?

TAKING IT FURTHER

Units 1–10 introduced some very basic terminology and concepts that are accepted and used in almost any serious discussion of word meaning. They are explained and discussed in the standard textbooks on semantics, though these generally devote more space to the discussion of 'sentence meaning' (which hasn't really been on our agenda at all in this book). The following are especially good general introductions: Hofmann (1993), Lyons (1995) and Palmer (1976/1981). A more thorough two-volume introduction is Allan (1986). Lyons (1977) is the classic survey of almost every issue in semantics, which all experts take as their starting-point, and is also in two volumes.

For introductions to the study of word meaning there is less choice. Of these, Jackson (1988) is mainly about dictionaries and the part played in them by definitions. Cruse (1986) is a very thorough exploration of the foundations on which the study of word meaning rests, with excellent discussions in depth of many issues that we have had to skate over in this course. Meaning change is discussed in any book on language change (including Trask (1994), in this series), but the most fun is to be had with a good etymological dictionary, such as Partridge (1958/1966). Aitchison (1987) is a very readable introduction to the psychological assumptions behind the course – in particular, to the idea that we store word meanings in our minds as a vast network of related concepts. Chapter 14 of Jackendoff (1993) is a readable and interesting introduction to the 'cognitive' approach that I have taken throughout this book; the rest of the book situates it in the context of much deeper issues.

Some of these issues are very profound indeed, and involve major controversy. Perhaps the most obvious example is the question of what our concepts are really like, which I raised in the unit on 'Typicality' (**Unit 4**). In arguing that concepts are based on clear cases, I was following a recent trend called (rather over-ambitiously, perhaps) 'Prototype theory'. This general view of concepts has been

REFERENCES

Aitchison, Jean (1987) *Words in the Mind*, Oxford: Blackwell.

Allan, Keith (1986) *Linguistic Meaning*, London: Routledge.

Burling, Robbins (1970) *Man's Many Voices: Language in its Cultural Context*, New York: Holt, Rinehart & Winston.

Cruse, D. Alan (1986) *Lexical Semantics*, Cambridge: Cambridge University Press.

Hofmann, Thomas (1993) *Realms of Meaning: An Introduction to Semantics*, London: Longman.

Hudson, Richard (1990) *English Word Grammar*, Oxford: Blackwell.

Jackendoff, Ray (1993) *Patterns in the Mind: Language and Human Nature*, New York: Harvester.

Jackson, Howard (1988) *Words and their Meaning*, London: Longman.

Lakoff, George (1987) *Women, Fire and Dangerous Things: What Categories Reveal about the Mind*, Chicago: University of Chicago Press.

Lehrer, Adrienne (1974) *Semantic Fields and Lexical Structure*, Amsterdam: North Holland.

Lyons, John (1977) *Semantics*, Cambridge: Cambridge University Press.

——(1995) *Linguistic Semantics: An Introduction*, Cambridge: Cambridge University Press.

Palmer, Frank (1976/1981) *Semantics: A New Outline*, 2nd edn, Cambridge: Cambridge University Press.

Partridge, Eric (1958/1966) *Origins*, London: Routledge.

Taylor, John (1989) *Linguistic Categorisation: An Essay in Cognitive Linguistics*, Oxford: Oxford University Press.

Trask, Larry (1994) *Language Change*, London: Routledge.

APPENDIX

NOUNS

ADULT
AEROPLANE
AUTHOR
BEGINNING
BIKE
BIT
BITCH
BREAKFAST
BULL
BUS
CAR
CHEF
CITY
CONNECTION
COOK
COW
CRICKET
DOE
DOG
END
ENEMY
EXPERT
FAMILY
FINGER
FRIEND
GAME

GANDER
GOOSE
GROWN-UP
IMPLEMENT
INGREDIENT
LENGTH
LINK
LONDON
MEAL
MEANING
MISTAKE
MOTHER
MUMMY
NAPKIN
NEIGHBOUR
NURSE
OAK
OPPOSITE
PEACOCK
PEAHEN
PIECE
PLACE
PLANE
PLANT
POTATO
PROFESSOR

RABBIT
RELATIVE
ROBBER
ROSE
RUNNER
SCREWDRIVER
SERVIETTE
SKATE
SLEDGE
SLIP
SLIPPER
SOLICITOR
SPOKE
SPUD
SQUARE-ROOT
TAILOR
TEACHER
THIEF
TOOL
TOP
TRAIN
TREE
UNIVERSITY
VEHICLE
WAITER
WAITRESS

VERBS

ANNOUNCE	GOSSIP	RING
ASCEND	GRUMBLE	RISE
ATTEMPT	HEAT	SCREAM
BABBLE	HISS	SCREECH
BAKE	HOLD	SCRIBBLE
BAWL	KILL	SHOUT
BELLOW	LEAVE	SHRINK
BITE	LECTURE	SINK
BOAST	LIKE	SLIDE
BOIL	MAKE	SPEAK
CHAT	MELT	STEAM
CHATTER	MOVE	TALK
CONTRACT	MUMBLE	TEST
COOK	MUNCH	THAW
DANCE	MURMUR	TRY
DIE	MUTTER	WALK
DRIVE	PHONE	WATCH
DROWN	PLAY	WHISPER
EAT	POACH	WRITE
FIND	POISON	YELL
FRY	REACH	
GET	READ	

INDEX